HEATHCLIFF
ALL AMERICAN

The funniest feline in America delights millions of fans every day as he appears in over 500 newspapers. You'll have a laugh a minute as Heathcliff tangles with the milkman, the cat show judge, the veterinarian and just about everyone else he runs into. If you're looking for some fun, look no further. Heathcliff is here!

Heathcliff Books

HEATHCLIFF
HEATHCLIFF RIDES AGAIN
HEATHCLIFF TRIPLE THREAT
HEATHCLIFF WANTED
HEATHCLIFF SPINS A YARN
HEATHCLIFF DOES IT AGAIN!
HEATHCLIFF STRIKES AGAIN!
HEATHCLIFF ROUND 3
HEATHCLIFF PIGS OUT
HEATHCLIFF FIRST PRIZE!
HEATHCLIFF'S TREASURE CHEST OF PUZZLES
HEATHCLIFF'S PUZZLERS
HEATHCLIFF PUZZLE SLEUTH
HEATHCLIFF BANQUET
HEATHCLIFF FEAST
SWEET SAVAGE HEATHCLIFF
WICKED LOVING HEATHCLIFF
HEATHCLIFF IN CONCERT
HEATHCLIFF PLAY BY PLAY
HEATHCLIFF DINES OUT
HEATHCLIFF GONE FISHIN'
HEATHCLIFF CLEANS HOUSE
HEATHCLIFF WORKING OUT
HEATHCLIFF CATCH OF THE DAY
HEATHCLIFF ON VACATION
HEATHCLIFF KOOL KAT
HEATHCLIFF ROCKIN' AND ROLLIN'
HEATHCLIFF SMOOTH SAILING
HEATHCLIFF ALL AMERICAN

HEATHCLIFF ALL AMERICAN!

by Geo Gately

JOVE BOOKS, NEW YORK

Originally included in the Tempo Books
collection *Heathcliff in Concert*.

HEATHCLIFF ALL AMERICAN

A Jove Book / published by arrangement with
Licensed Ventures, International.

PRINTING HISTORY
Special Book Club edition / April 1987

All rights reserved.
Copyright © 1978, 1979, 1980 by McNaught Syndicate, Inc.
This book may not be reproduced in whole or in part,
by mimeograph or any other means, without permission.
For information address: The Berkley Publishing Group,
200 Madison Avenue, New York, New York 10016.

Jove Books are published by The Berkley Publishing Group,
200 Madison Avenue, New York, New York 10016.
The name "JOVE" and the "J" logo
are trademarks belonging to Jove Publications, Inc.

PRINTED IN THE UNITED STATES OF AMERICA

10   9   8   7   6   5   4   3   2   1

WET CEMENT
2-13
© 1980 McNaught Synd., Inc.
"IT MUST HAVE BEEN A MONSTER!"

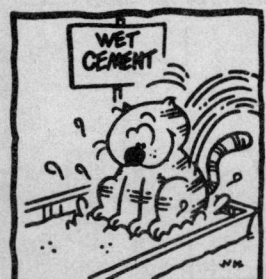

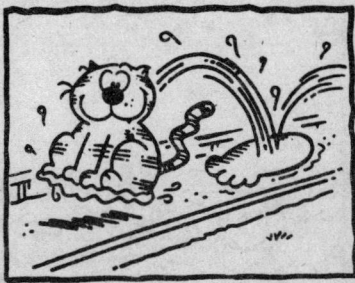

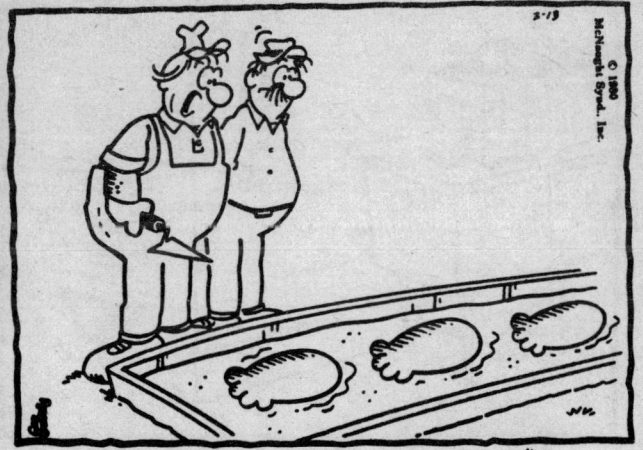

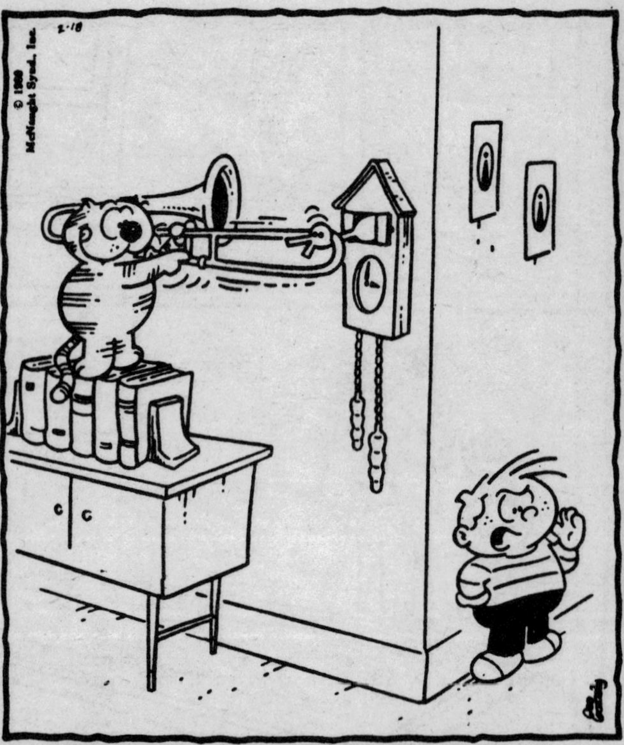
2·18
McNaught Synd., Inc.

"HEATHCLIFF!...WHERE'S MY TROMBONE ?!"

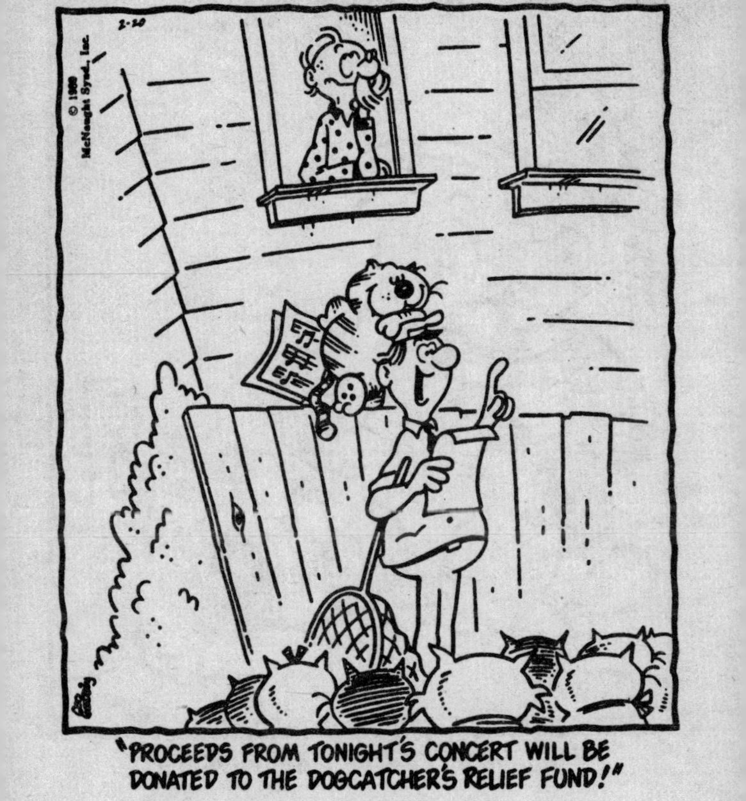
McNaught Synd., Inc.
2-20

"PROCEEDS FROM TONIGHT'S CONCERT WILL BE DONATED TO THE DOGCATCHER'S RELIEF FUND!"

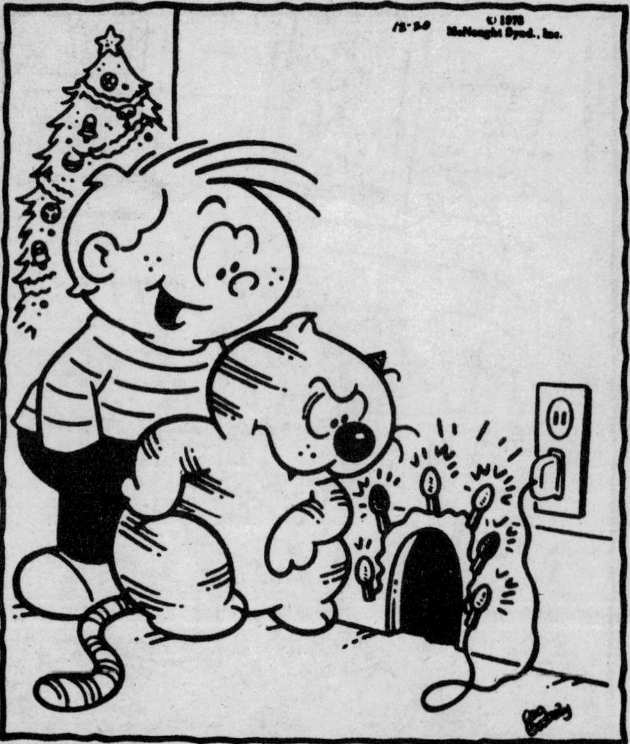
12-20
© 1978
McNaught Synd., Inc.

"THEY'VE DECORATED THEIR DOORWAY."

McNaught Synd., Inc.
2-22
TUNA FLEET
TUNA FLEET

"LEMME KNOW IF YE SPOT ANY TUNA."

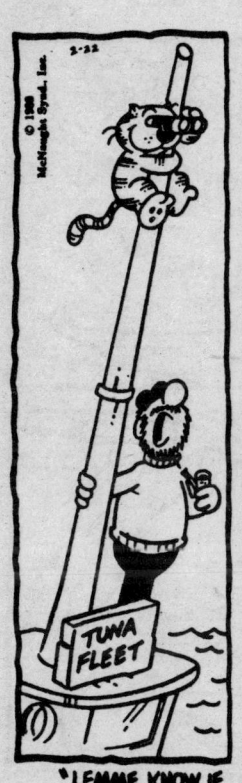

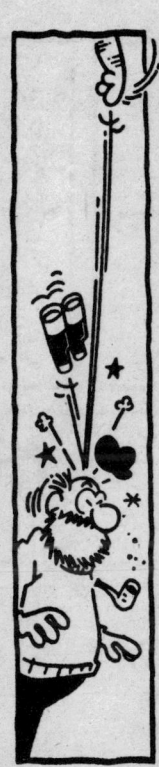

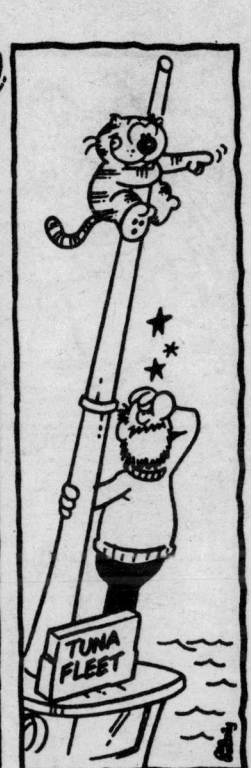

McNaught Synd., Inc.

"PHEW!...TALK ABOUT A SHOWER MASSAGE!!"

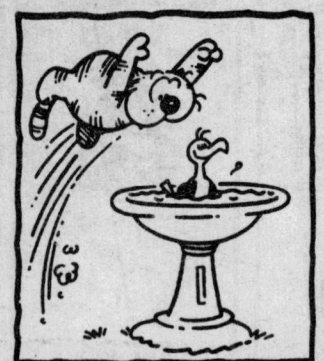

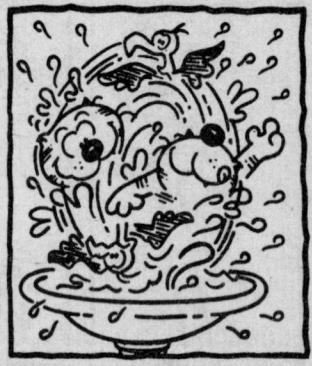

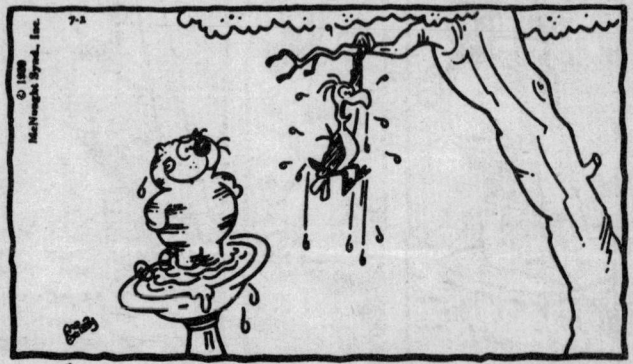

"ALL CLEAR!"

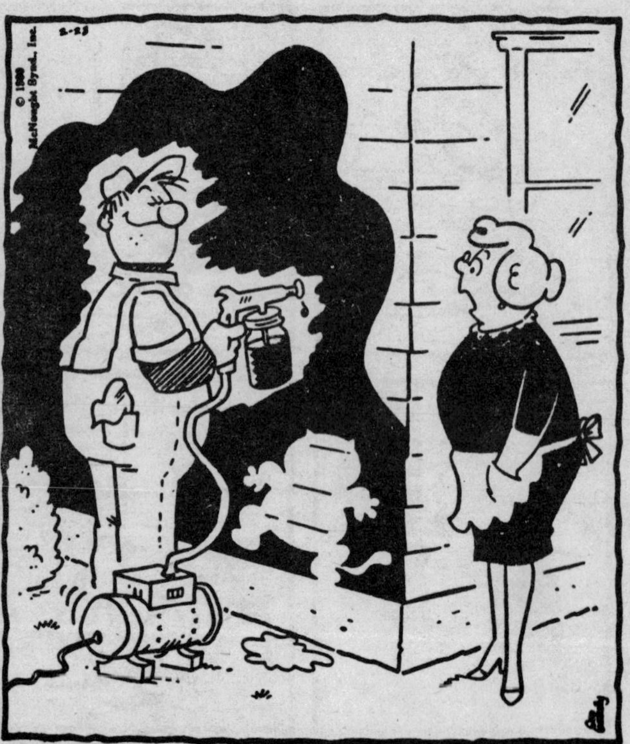
2-23
McNaught Synd., Inc.

"LET ME KNOW IF HEATHCLIFF ANNOYS YOU."

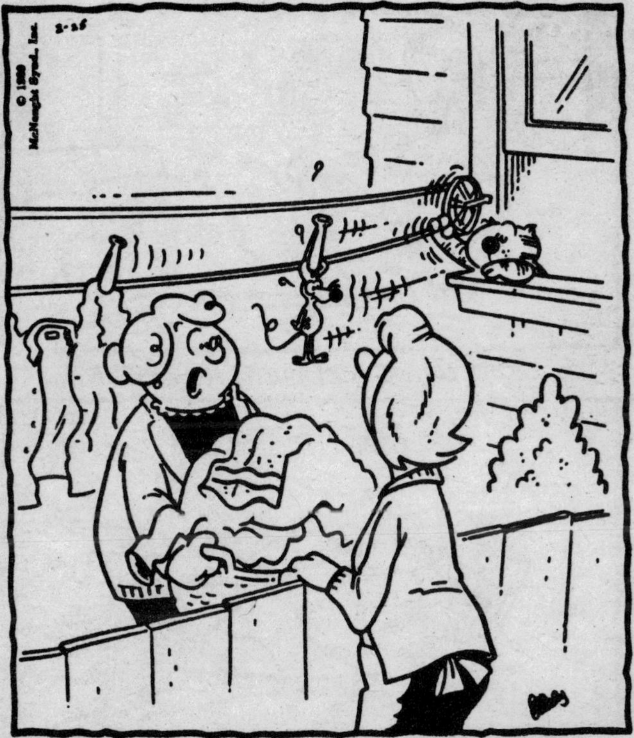
McNaught Synd., Inc.
2-26

"HEATHCLIFF'S BEEN CHASING A MOUSE ALL MORNING."

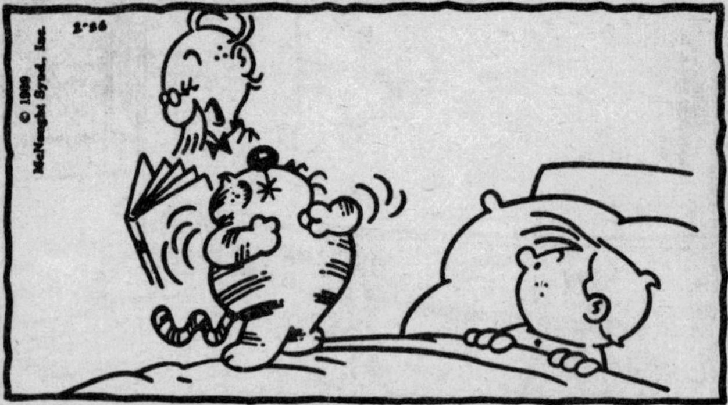
McNaught Synd., Inc.
2-26

"....SO, THE BIG, BAD WOLF HUFFED AND PUFFED AND....

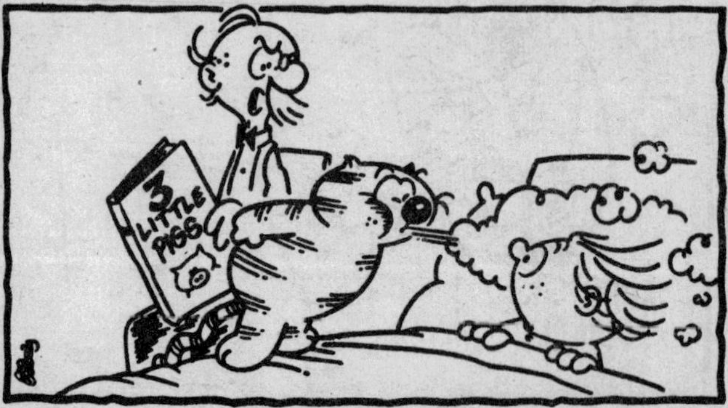
3 LITTLE PIGS

...I'LL TELL THE STORY!"

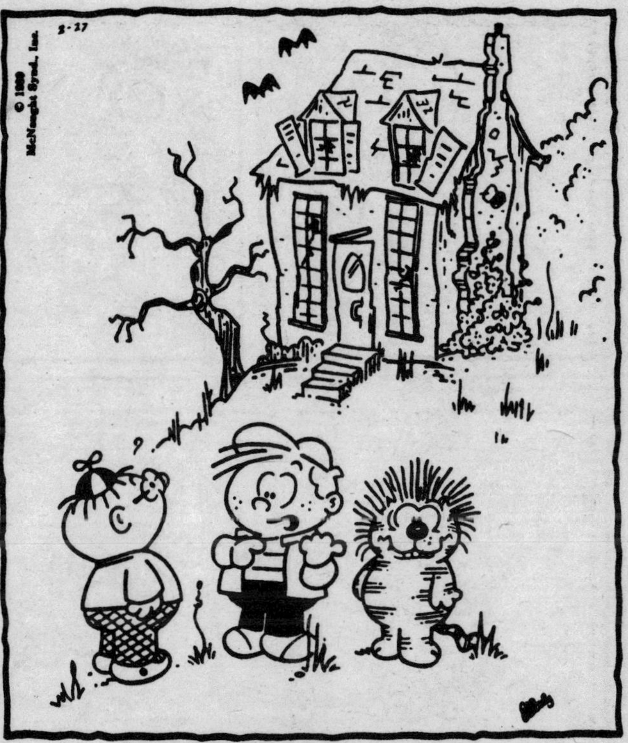
McNaught Synd., Inc.

"I THINK THE PLACE IS HAUNTED, AND SO DOES HEATHCLIFF!"

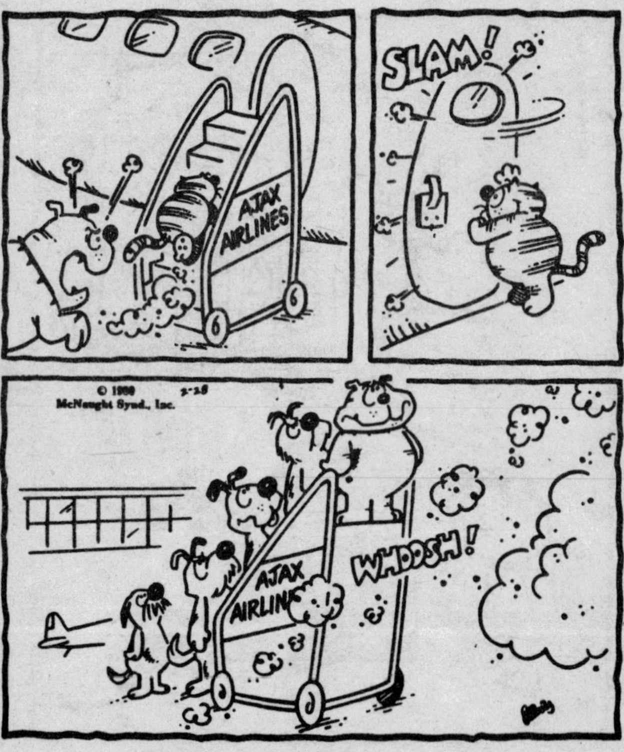
AJAX AIRLINES
SLAM!
© 1980
2-28
McNaught Synd., Inc.
AJAX AIRLINE
WHOOSH!

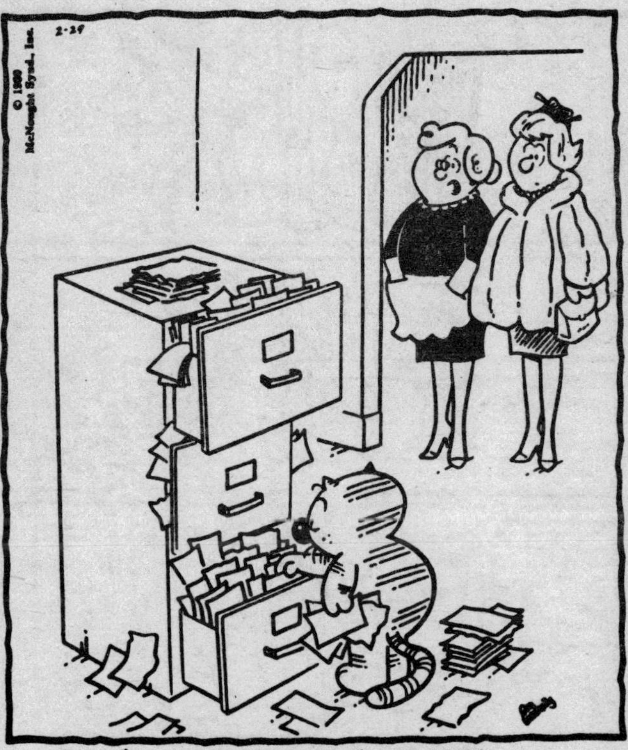
McNaught Synd., Inc.
2-29

"I FINALLY GOT HIM TO ORGANIZE
HIS CAT FOOD COUPONS."

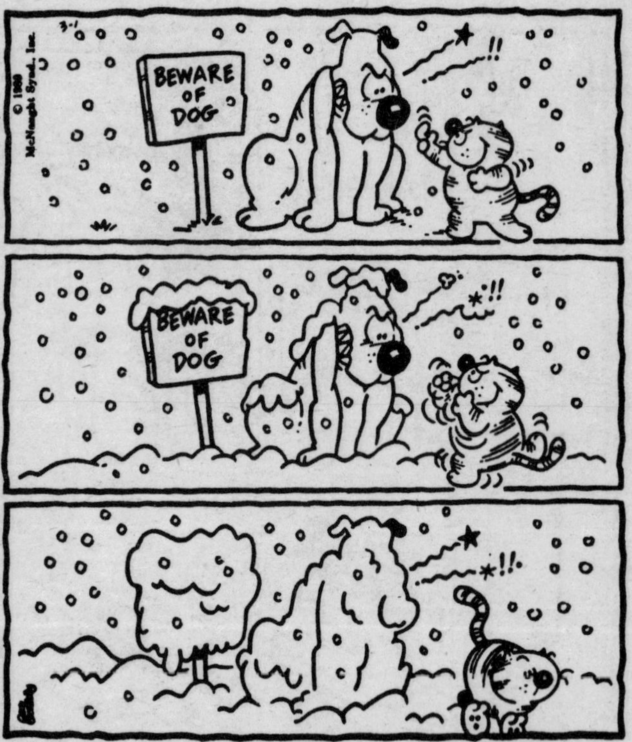
BEWARE OF DOG
!!
© 1988 McNaught Synd., Inc.
BEWARE OF DOG
!!
!!

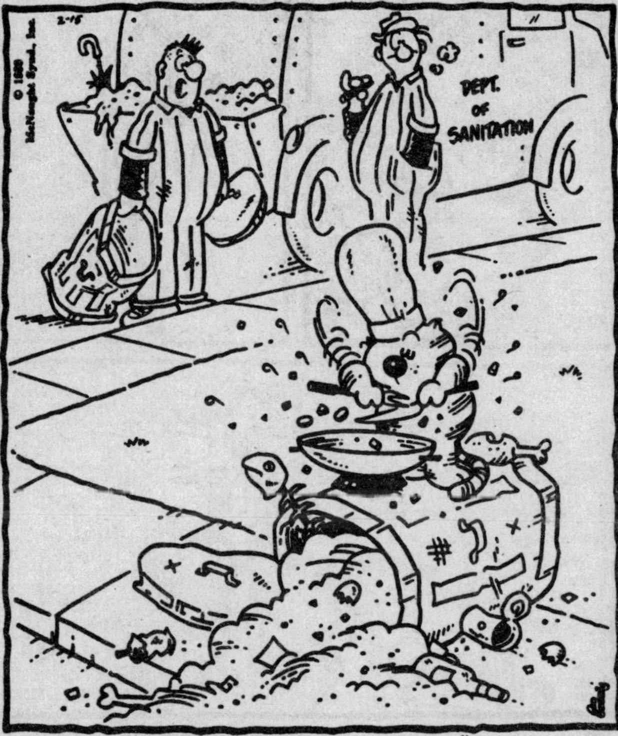

© 1986 McNaught Synd., Inc.
2-15
DEPT. OF SANITATION

"HE'S GOT HIMSELF A WOK!"

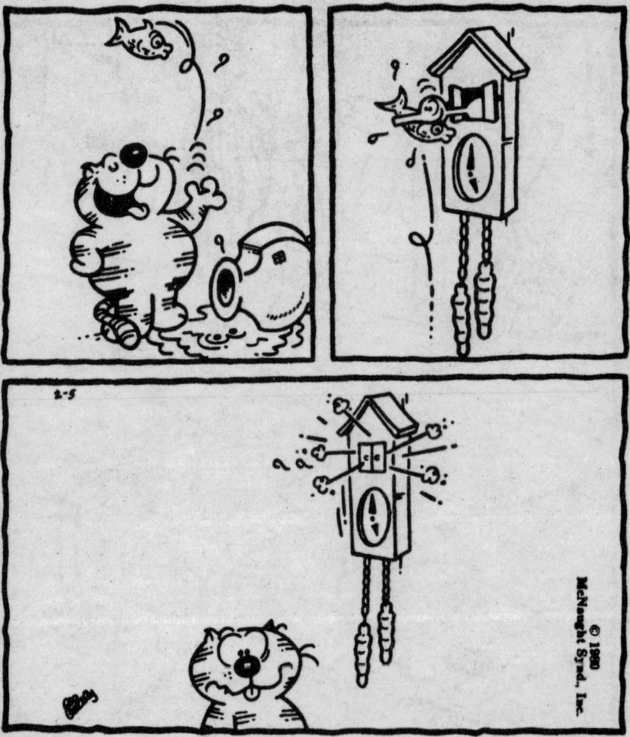
2-5
© 1980
McNaught Synd., Inc.

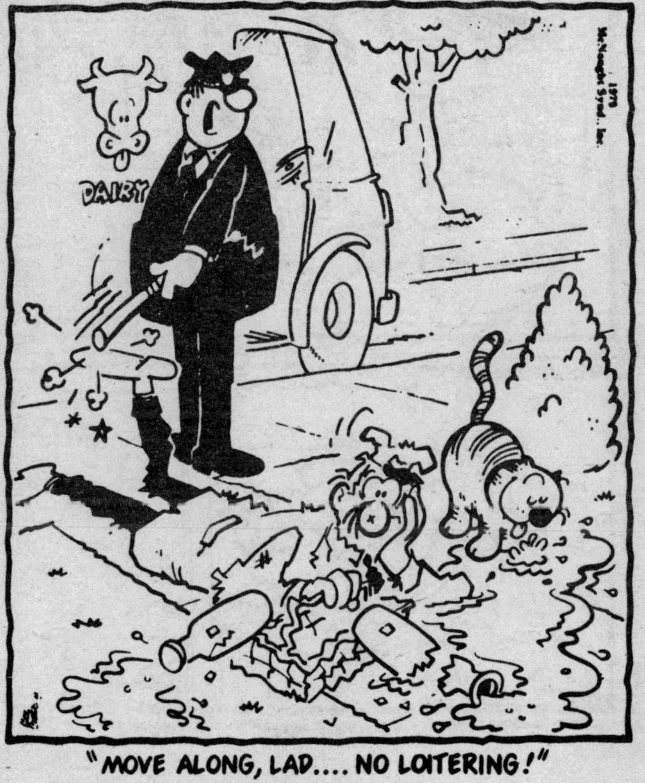
DAIRY

"MOVE ALONG, LAD.... NO LOITERING!"

"COME BACK WITH THAT FLOUNDER!"

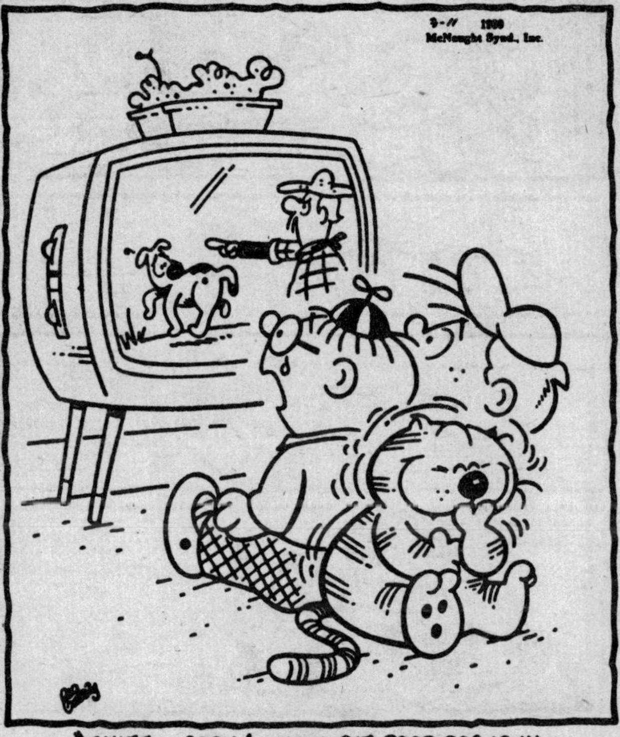
3-11 1980
McNaught Synd., Inc.

"SNIFF...GOSH!...NOW THE POOR DOG IS IN REAL TROUBLE!!"

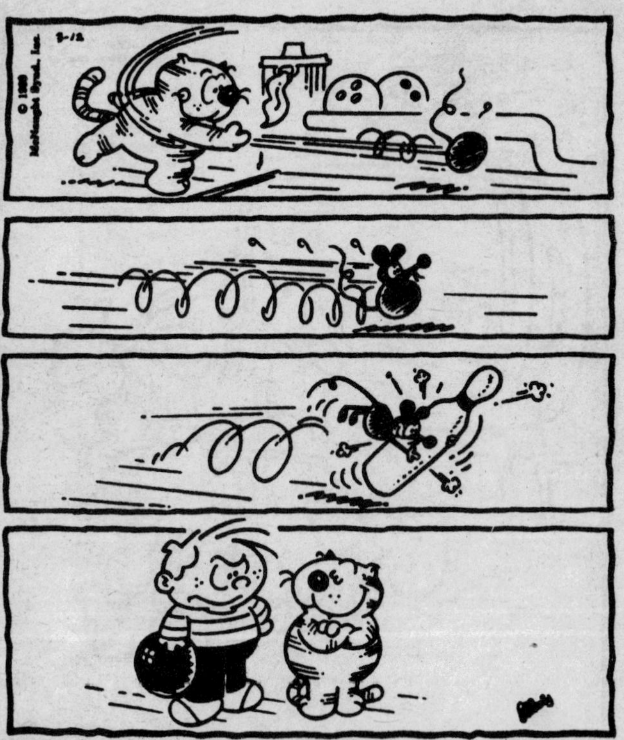
McNaught Synd., Inc.
3-12

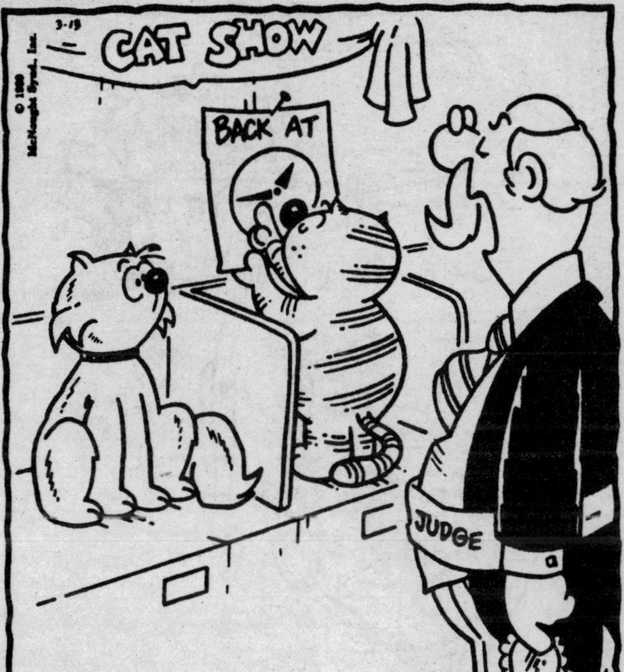
3-13
CAT SHOW
BACK AT
JUDGE

"CONTESTANTS WILL REMAIN IN THEIR BOOTHS!"

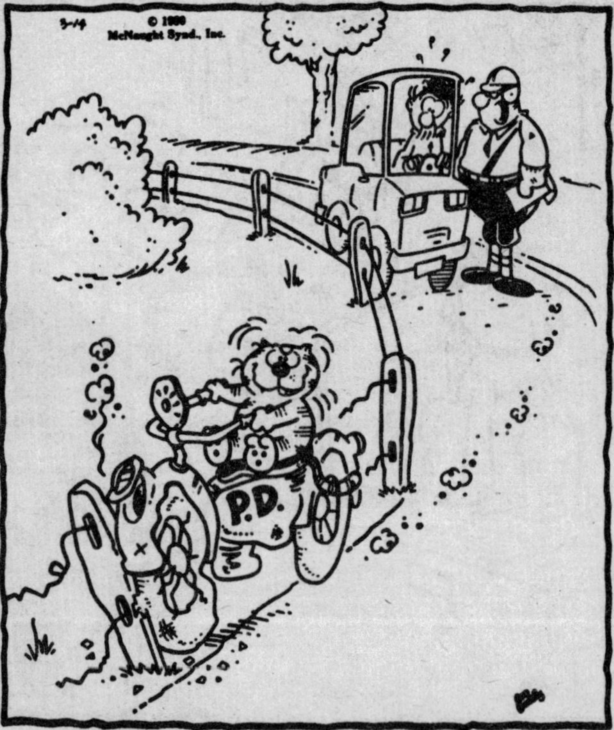
3-14
McNaught Synd., Inc.
P.D.

"HE'S NOT HELPING THIS SITUATION ANY!"

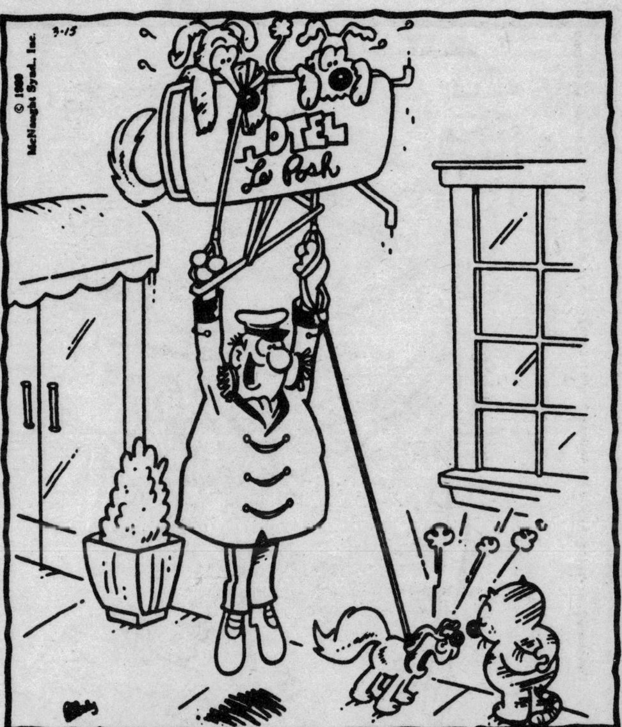
McNaught Synd., Inc.
HOTEL
Le Posh

"SEE THERE?... FIFI'S NOT AFRAID OF YOU!"

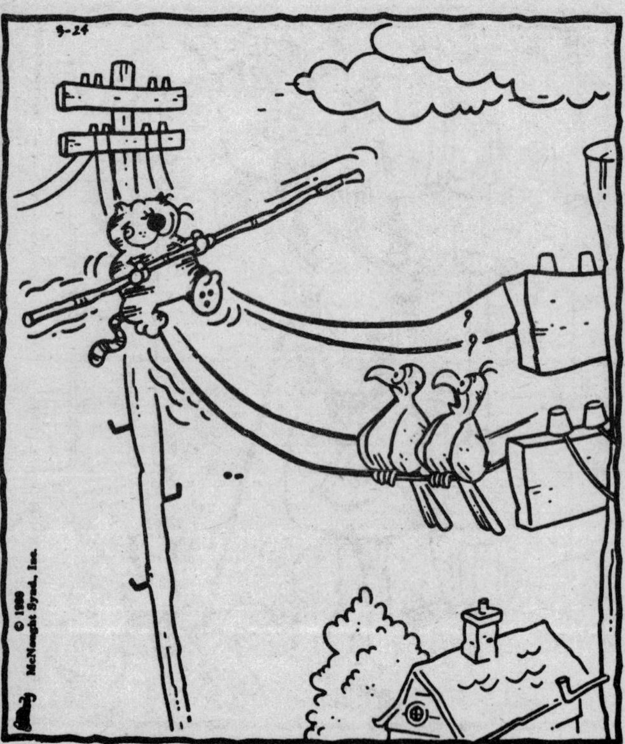
3-24
© 1980 McNaught Synd., Inc.

"HERE COMES OL' TWINKLETOES!"

McNaught Synd., Inc.
BLAM!

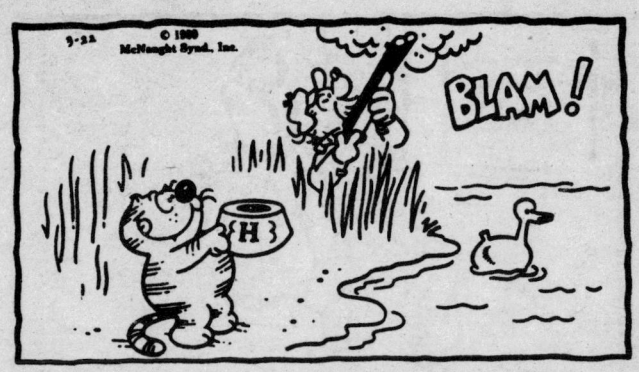

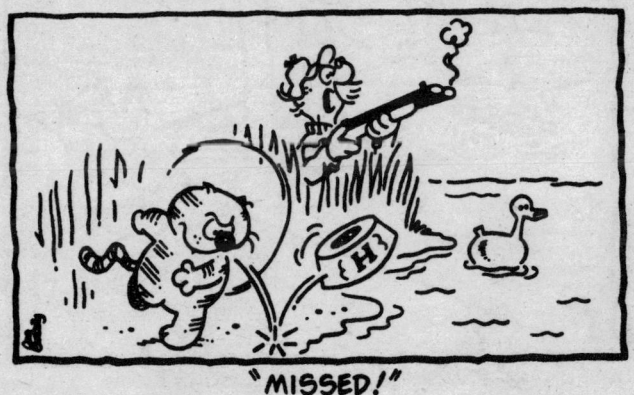

"MISSED!"

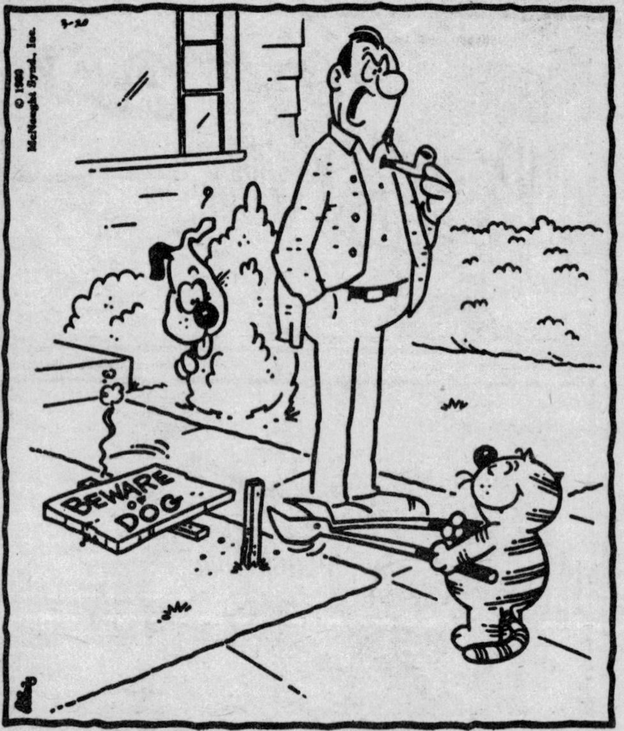
McNaught Synd., Inc.
3-20
BEWARE OF DOG

"PRUNING EARLY THIS SPRING?!"

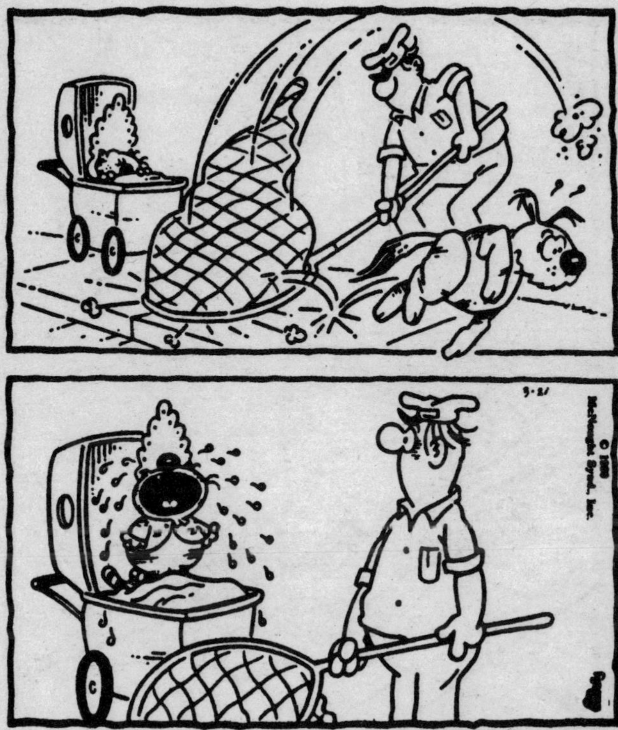
3-21
McNaught Synd., Inc.

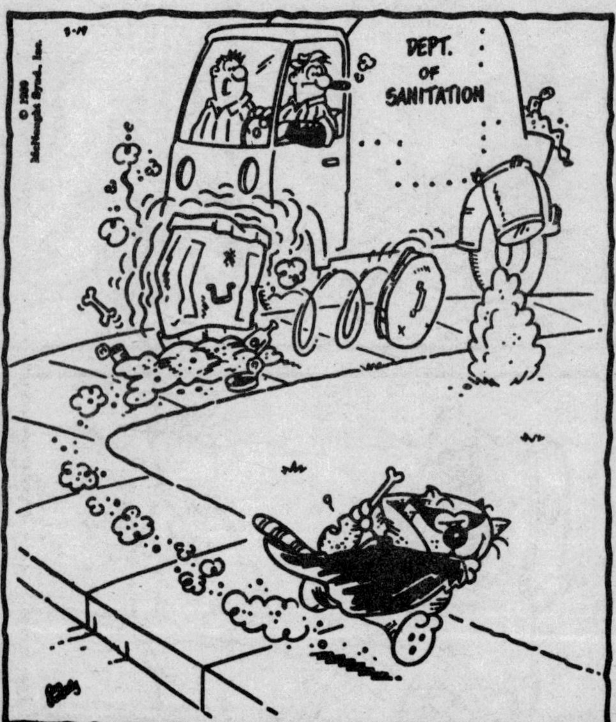
DEPT. OF SANITATION

"THE 'PHANTOM OF GARBAGE' STRIKES AGAIN!"

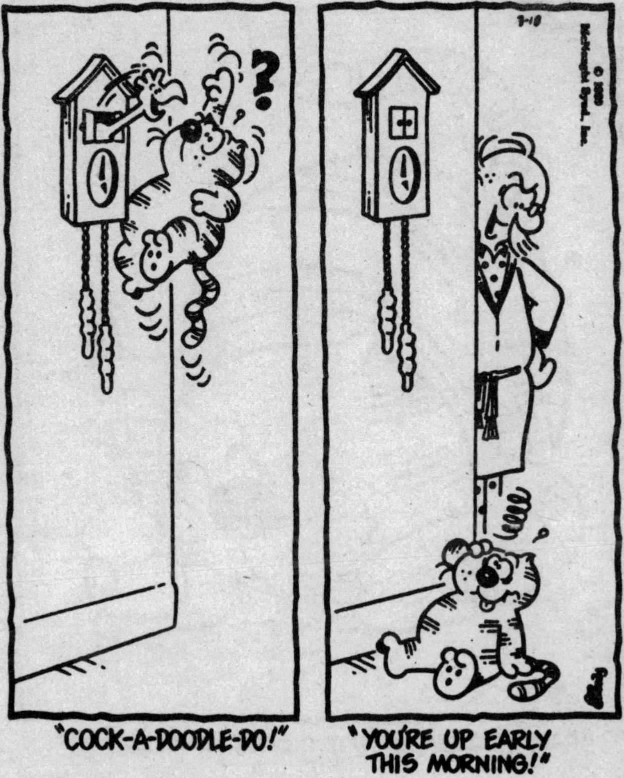
"COCK-A-DOODLE-DO!"
"YOU'RE UP EARLY THIS MORNING!"

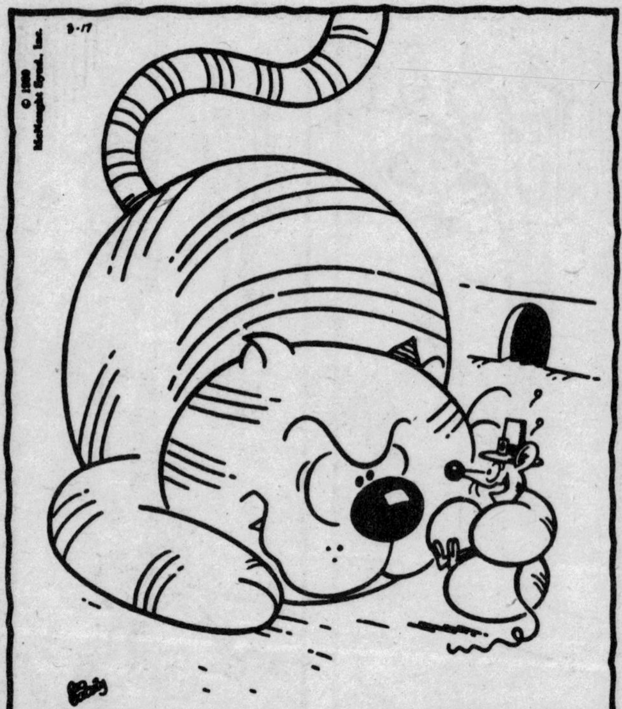
3-17

"HAVE YE NEVER HEARD O' THE WEE LEPRECHAUNS?"

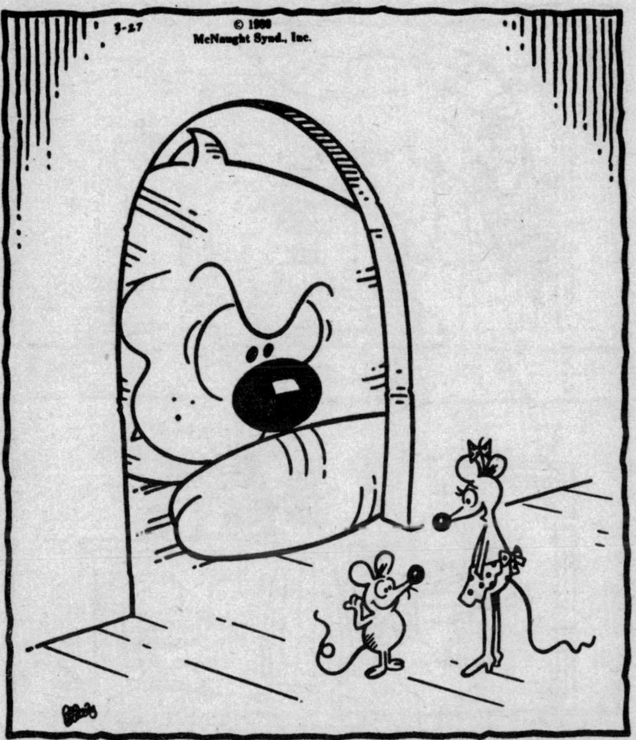
3-27
McNaught Synd., Inc.

"NO, DEAR... HE IS NOT WITH THE 'WELCOME WAGON'."

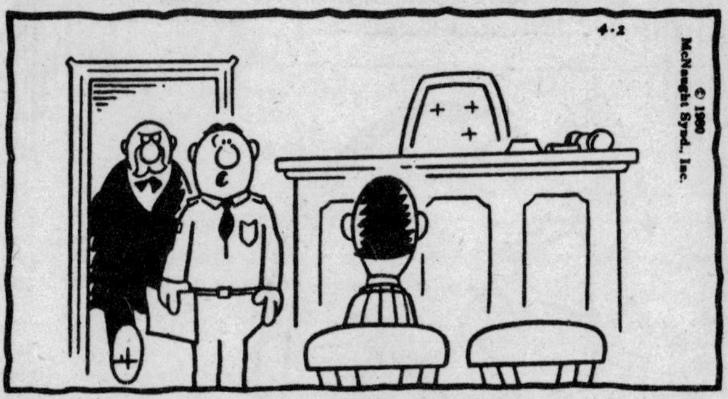
4-2
© 1980 McNaught Synd., Inc.

"ALL RISE...."

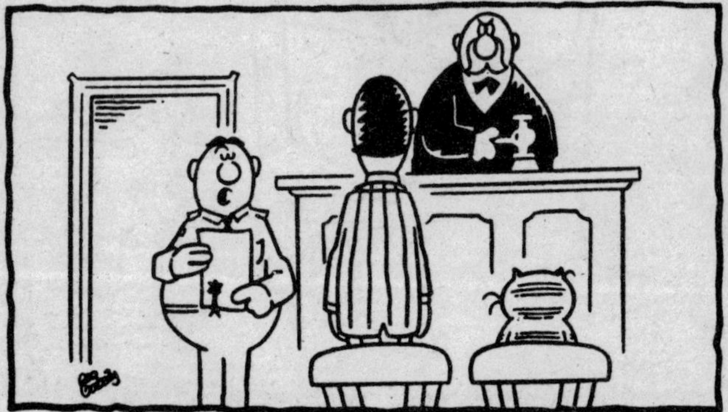

"THE STATE VERSUS HEATHCLIFF...."

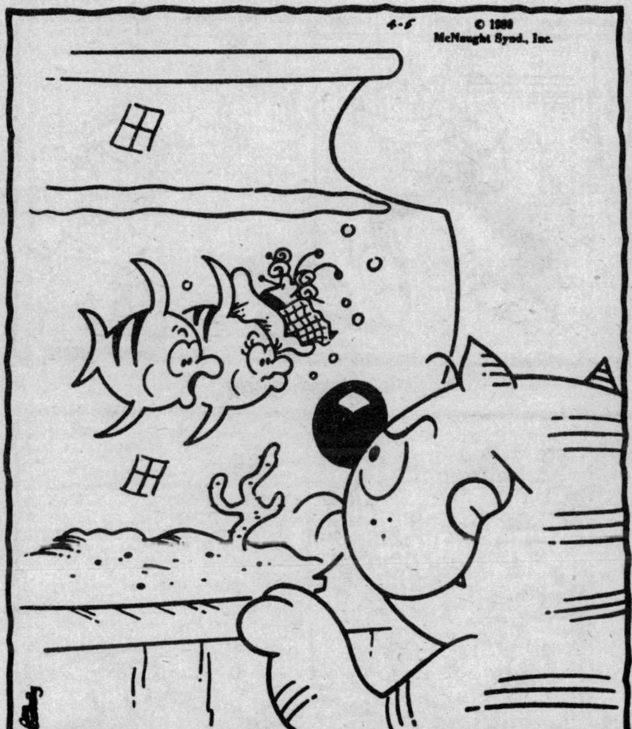
4-5
McNaught Synd., Inc.

"I DON'T THINK HE'S ADMIRING YOUR EASTER BONNET!"

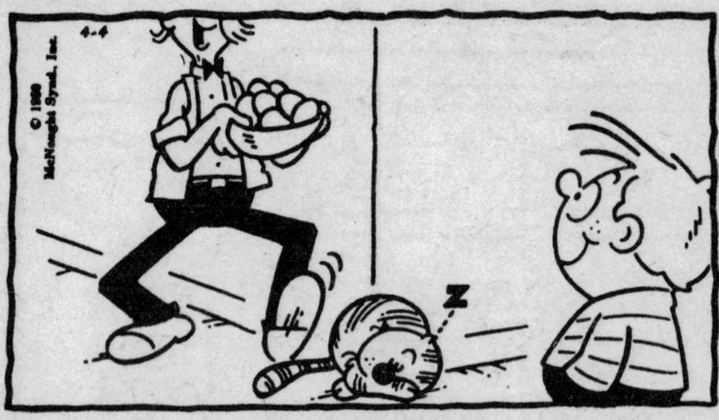
4-4
McNaught Synd., Inc.
Z

"LET'S COLOR SOME...

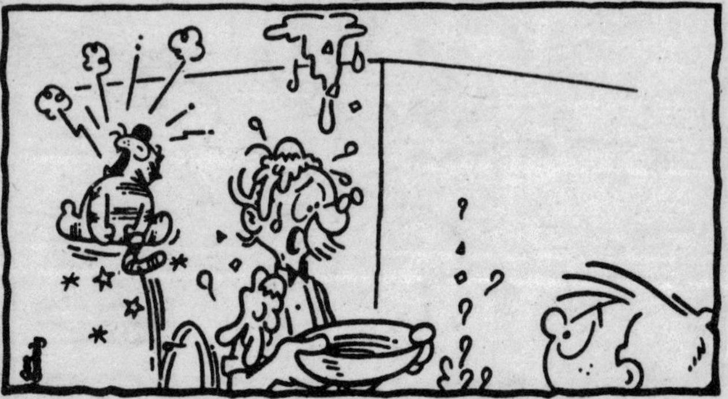

...EASTER EGGS."

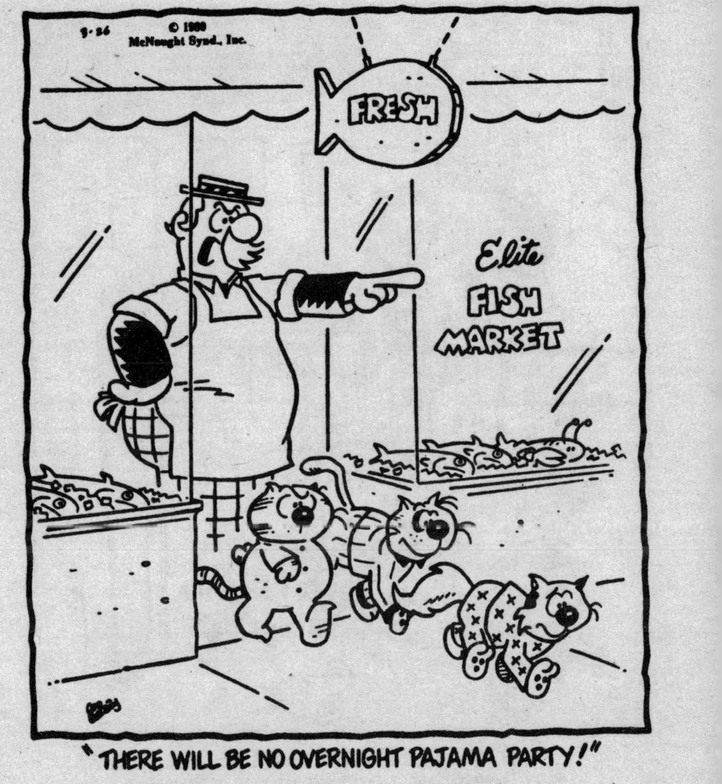
McNaught Synd., Inc.
FRESH
Elite
FISH
MARKET

"THERE WILL BE NO OVERNIGHT PAJAMA PARTY!"

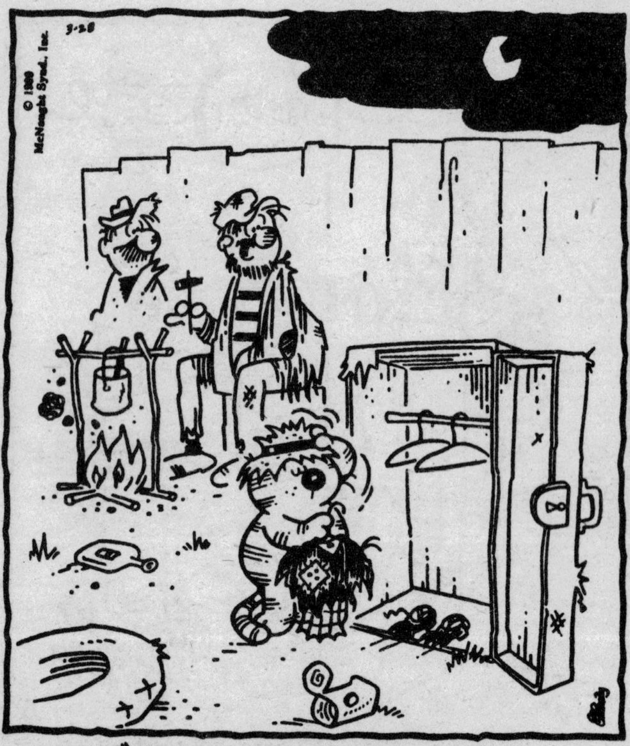
3-28
McNaught Synd., Inc.

"NOW AND THEN HE LEAVES HOME,
SO I KEEP HIS CLOTHES IN THE TRUNK."

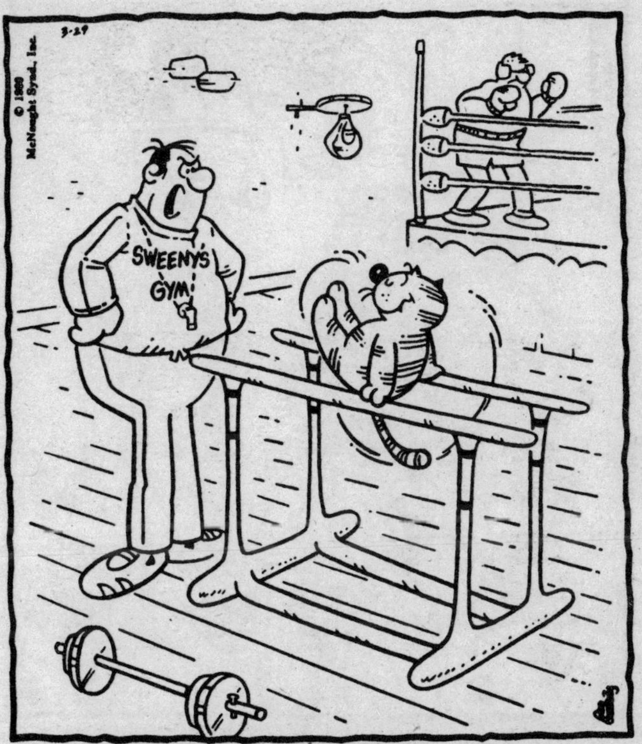
3-29
McNaught Synd., Inc.
SWEENY'S GYM

"YOU'RE SUPPOSED TO GET YOUR WORKOUT CHASING MICE!"

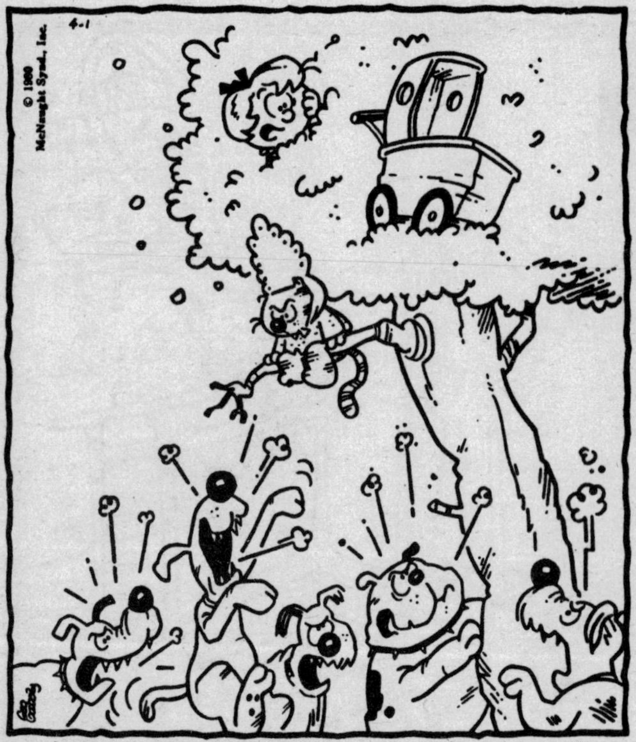
4-1
© 1980 McNaught Synd., Inc.

"PHEEW!...YOU SURE CAN CLIMB WHEN YOU WANT TO!"

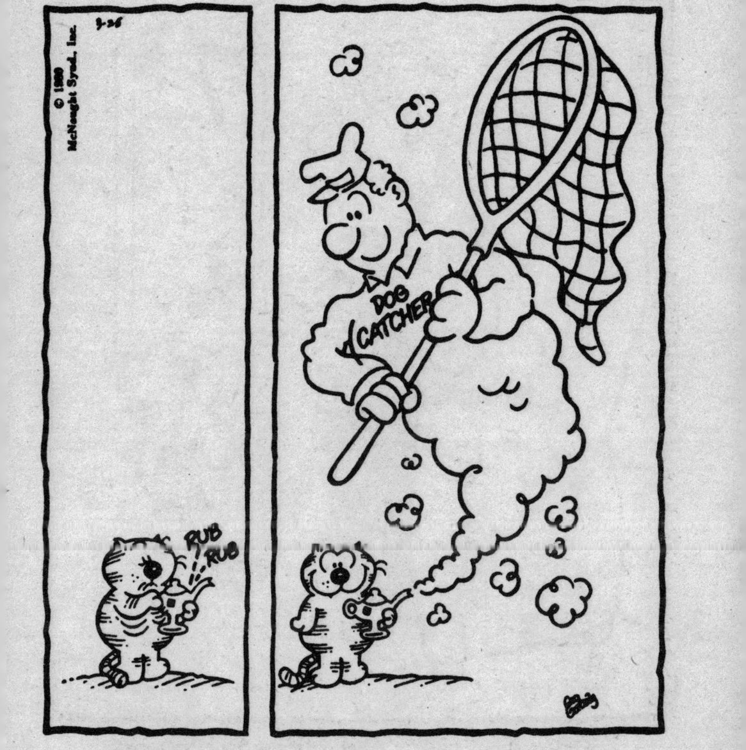
© 1980 McNaught Synd., Inc.
RUB RUB
DOG CATCHER

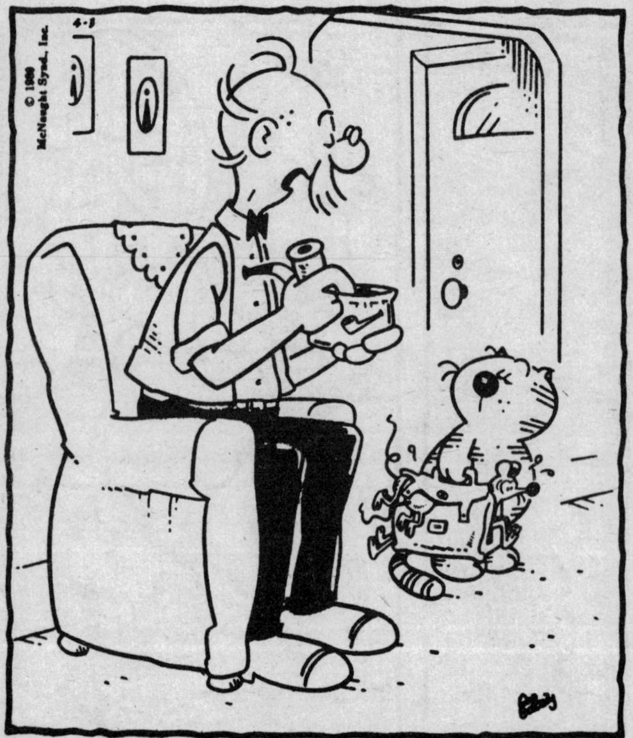
McNaught Synd., Inc.

"I WISH YOU'D LEAVE YOUR BUSINESS PROBLEMS AT THE OFFICE."

"FOILED BY A SCRATCHING POST!"

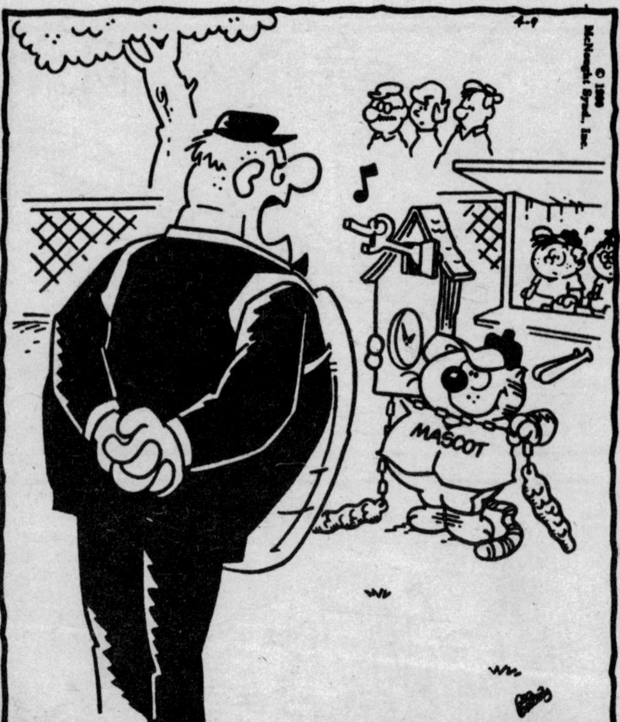
4-9
© 1986 McNaught Synd., Inc.
MASCOT

"I'VE HAD ENOUGH OF YOUR HECKLING!"

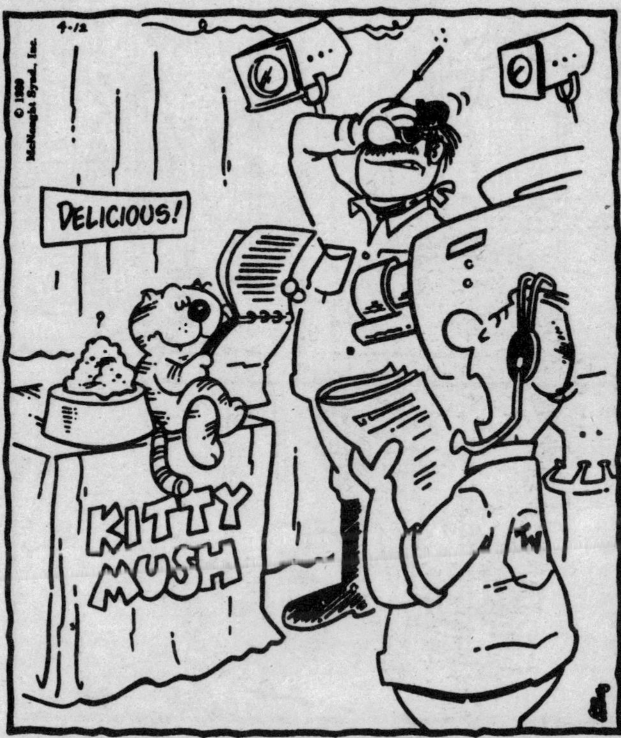
4-12
DELICIOUS!
?
KITTY MUSH
TW

"HIS CONTRACT GRANTS HIM SCRIPT APPROVAL."

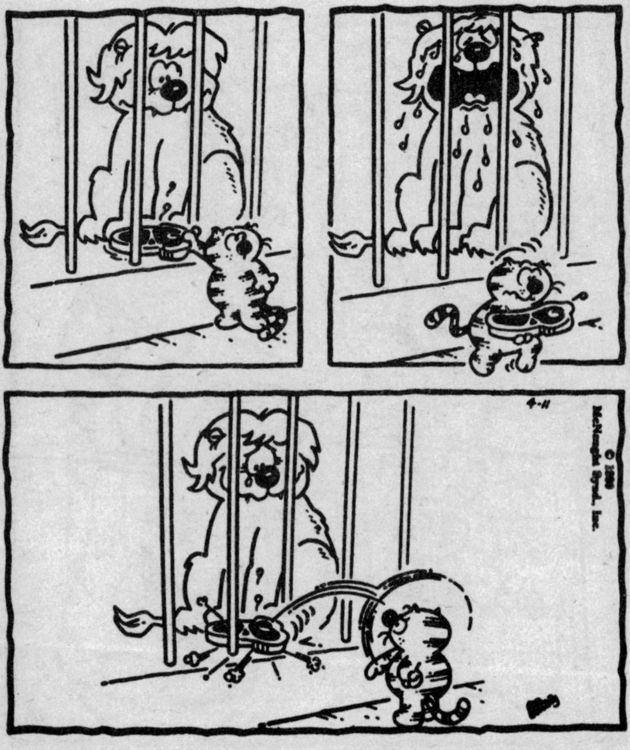
4-11
© McNaught Synd., Inc.

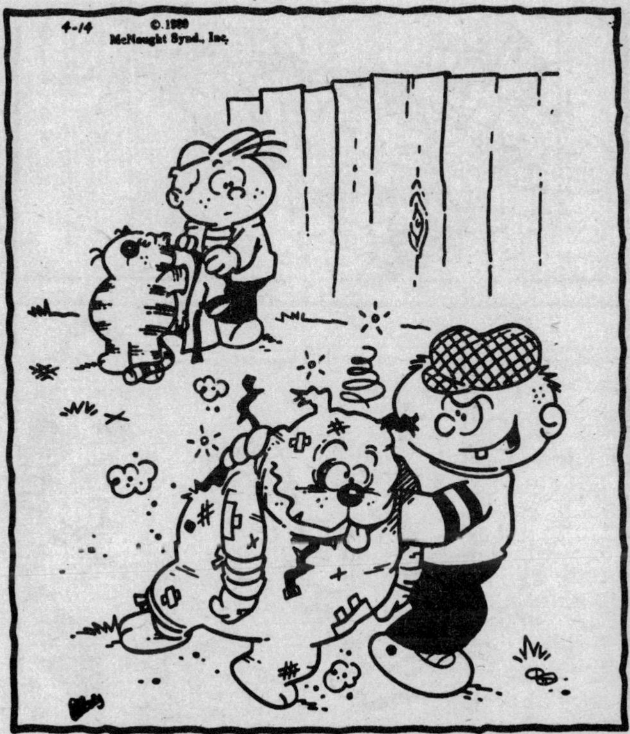
4-14
©.1989
McNaught Synd., Inc.

"NICE GOIN', SPIKE...YOU WENT THE DISTANCE!"

© 1986
McNaught Synd., Inc.
4-16

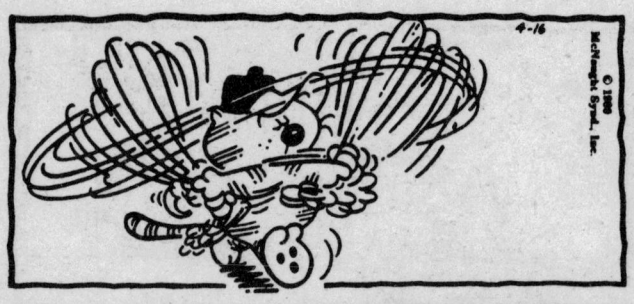

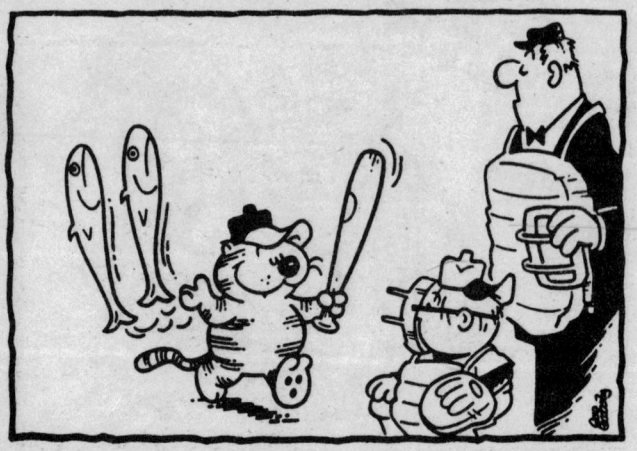

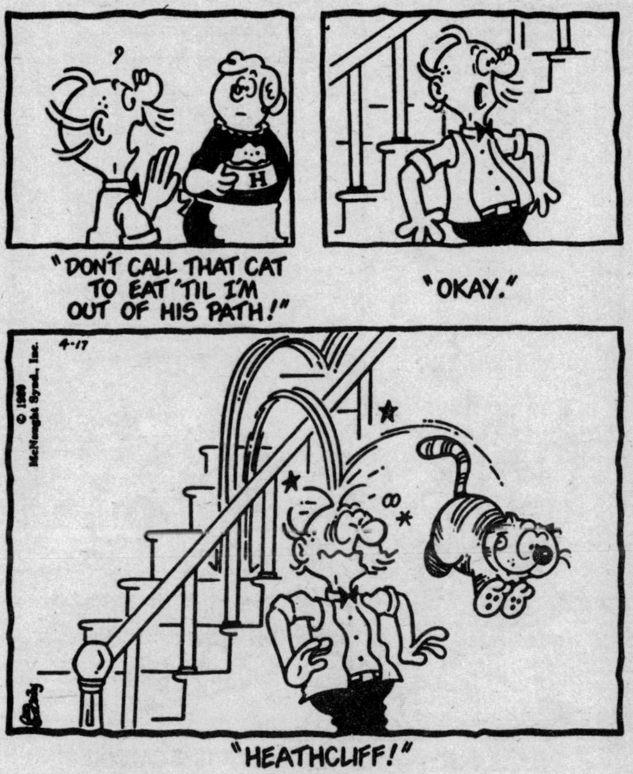
"DON'T CALL THAT CAT TO EAT 'TIL I'M OUT OF HIS PATH!"
"OKAY."
4-17
McNaught Synd., Inc.
"HEATHCLIFF!"

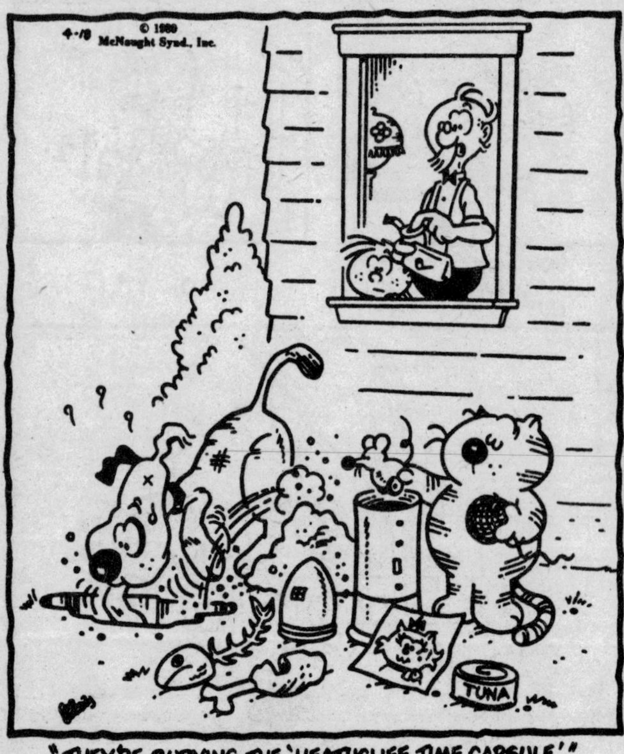
McNaught Synd., Inc.
TUNA

"THEY'RE BURYING THE 'HEATHCLIFF TIME CAPSULE'."

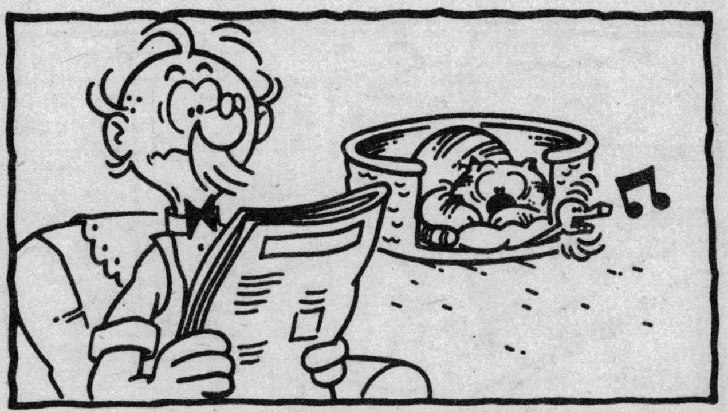

"COO, COO!"

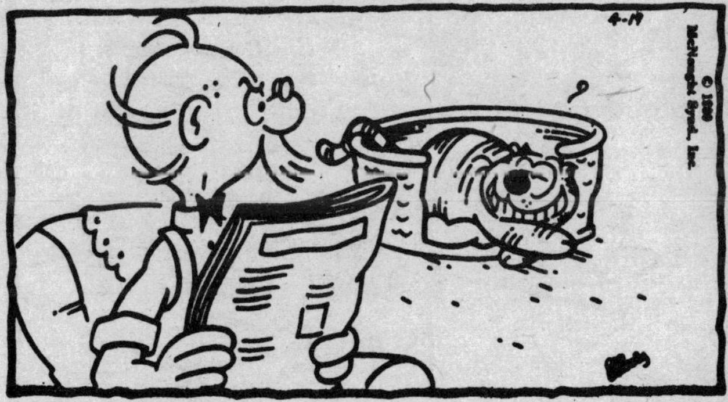

4-19
McNaught Synd., Inc.

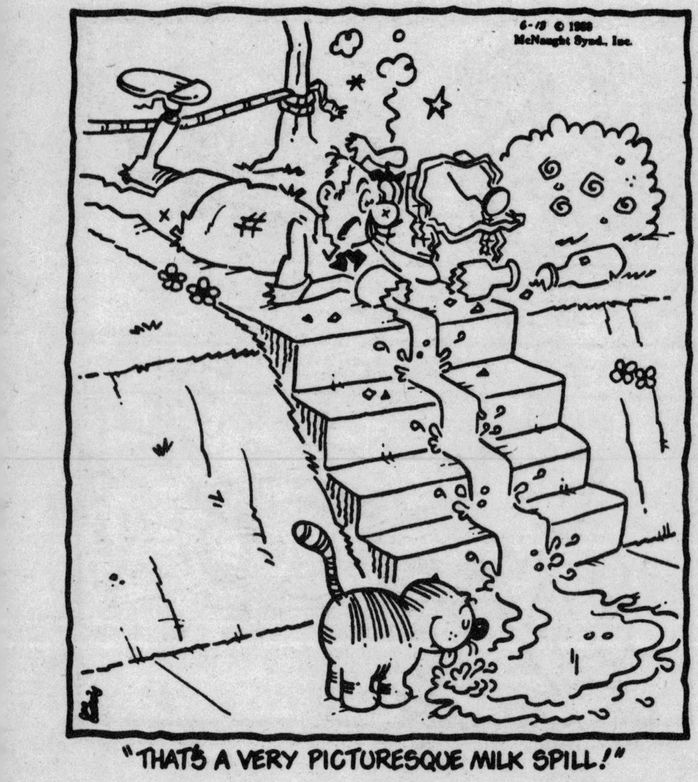
McNaught Synd., Inc.

"THAT'S A VERY PICTURESQUE MILK SPILL!"

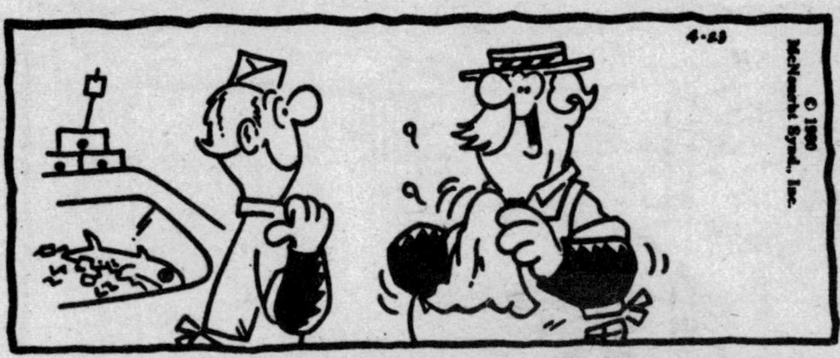
4-23
© 1980 McNaught Synd., Inc.

"A CONTRIBUTION?...CERTAINLY! WE'RE ALWAYS GLAD TO HELP THE CHILDREN'S HOME!"

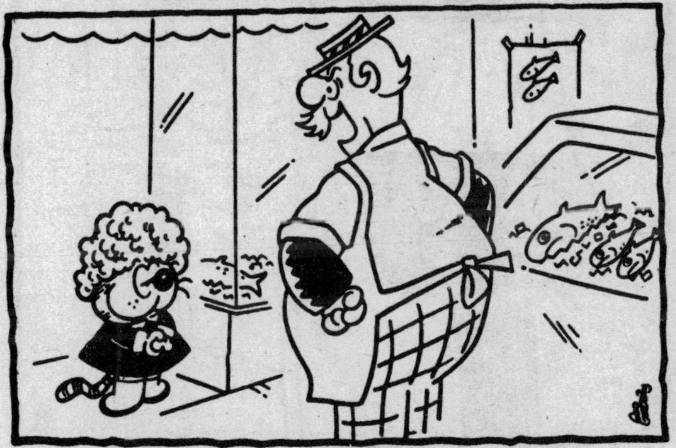

"WELL!...IF IT AIN'T 'LITTLE ORPHAN ANNIE'!"

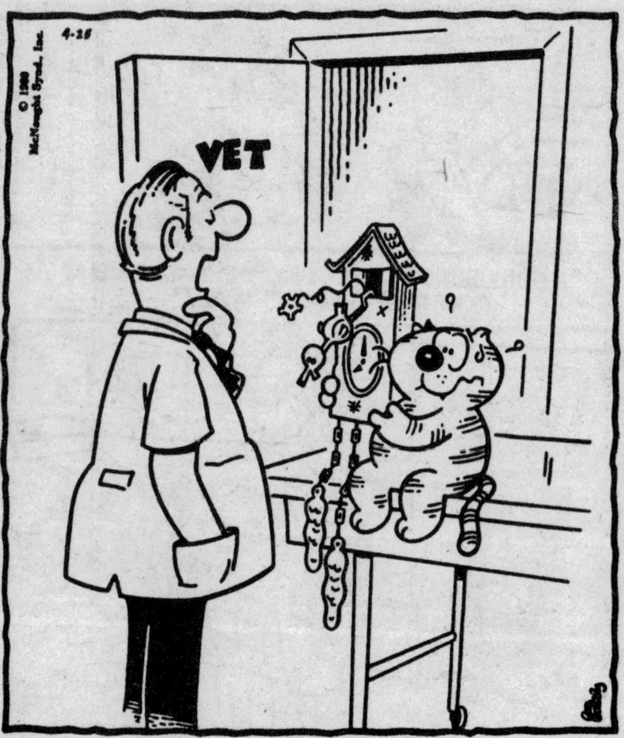
4-25
VET

"THAT'S A VERY SICK BIRD."

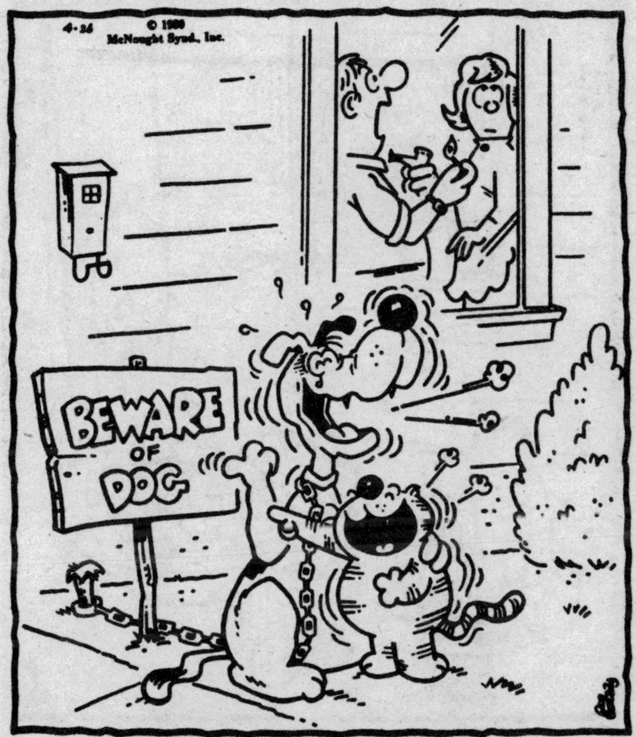
4-26
© 1980
McNaught Synd., Inc.
BEWARE
OF
DOG

"SOMEBODY IS HAVING A GOOD LAUGH ABOUT SOMETHING!"

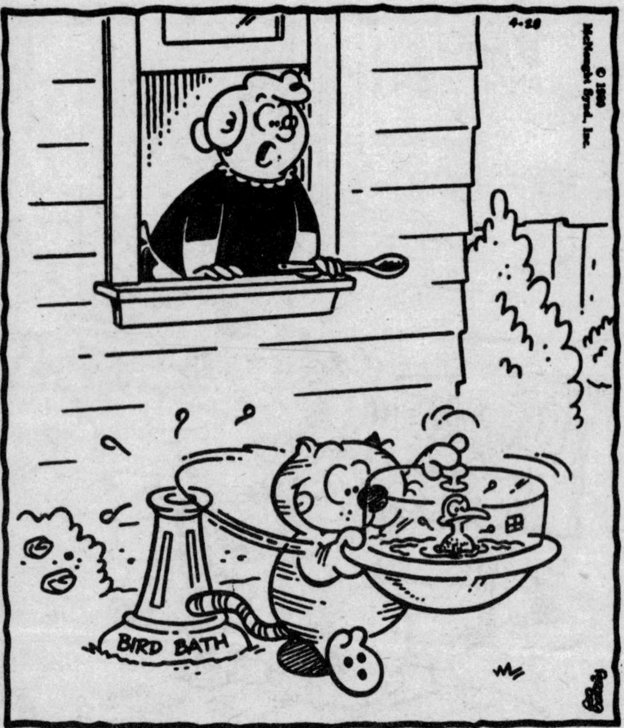
4-28
© 1980 McNaught Synd., Inc.
BIRD BATH

"HEATHCLIFF!...IS THAT THE TOP OF THE CAKE DISH?"

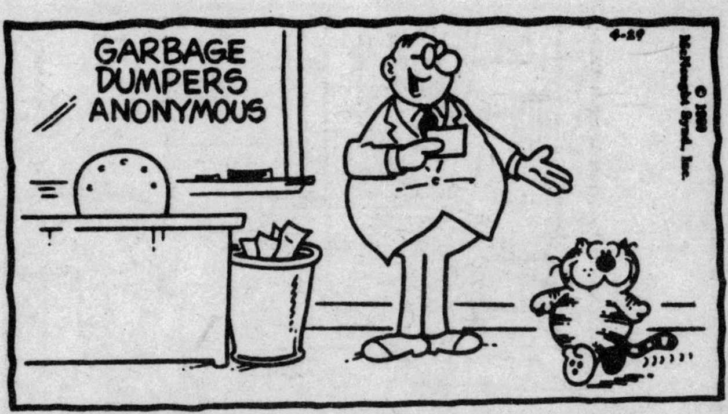
GARBAGE DUMPERS ANONYMOUS
4-29

"PLEASE WELCOME OUR NEWEST MEMBER, HEATHCLIFF...

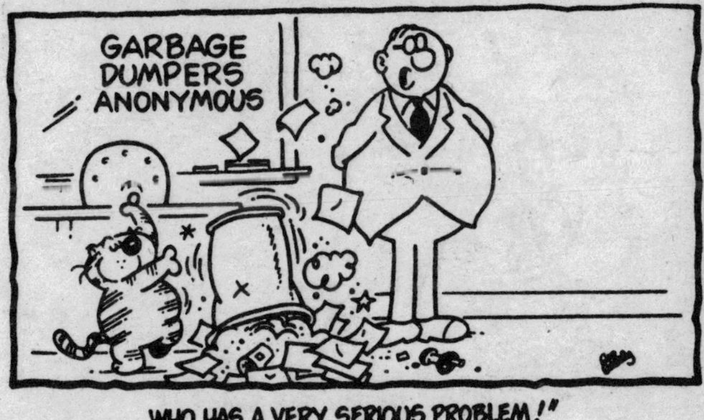
GARBAGE DUMPERS ANONYMOUS

...WHO HAS A VERY SERIOUS PROBLEM!"

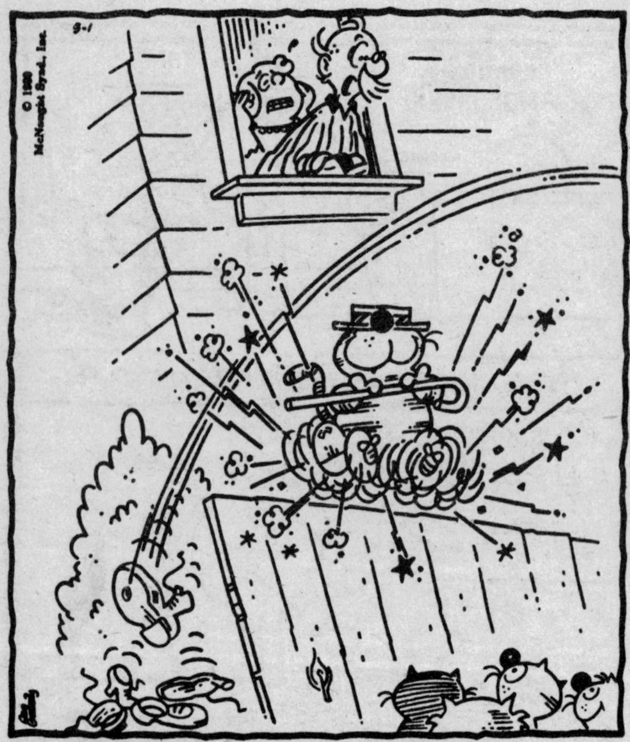
© 1986 McNaught Synd., Inc.
8-1

"SOMEBODY THREW TAP SHOES!"

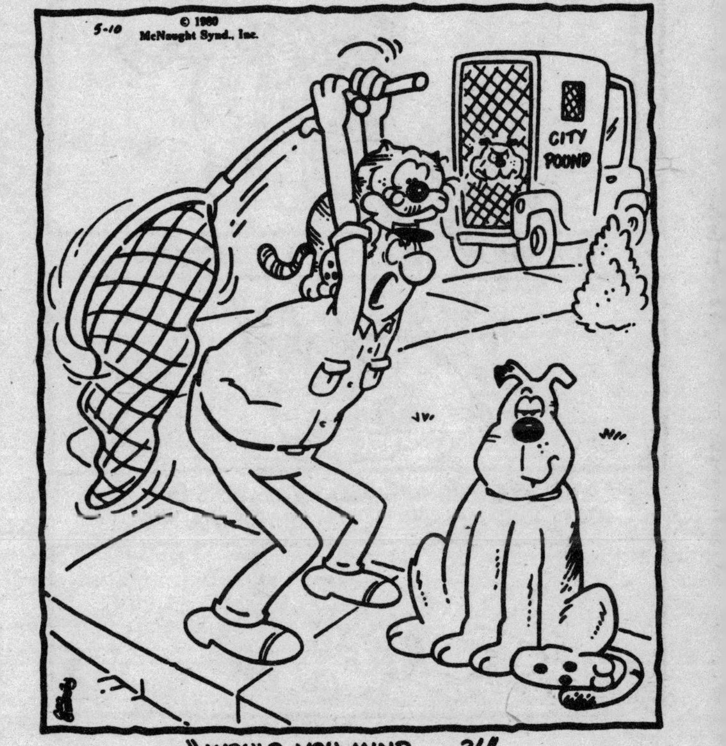
5-10
© 1980
McNaught Synd., Inc.
CITY
POUND

"WOULD YOU MIND.....?!"

"NOW, NOW, HEATHCLIFF... LET'S BE CHARITABLE!...

...LET'S BE FORGIVING, WHOLESOME, PURE OF HEART, KIND AND GENTLE, LOVING, MERCIFUL AND..."

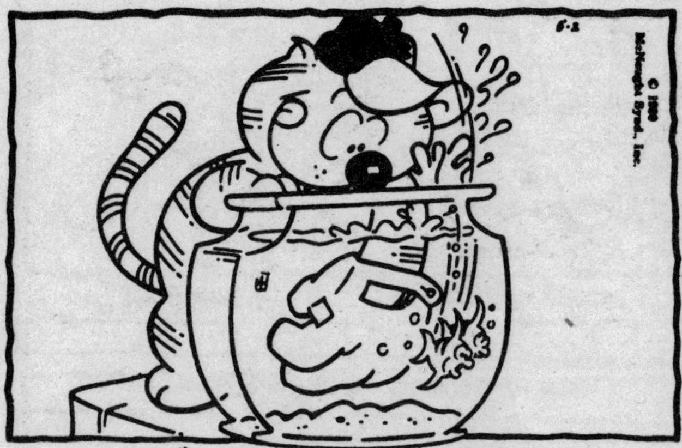
6·2
McNaught Synd., Inc.

"LOOK OUT!!...ITS...ITS...

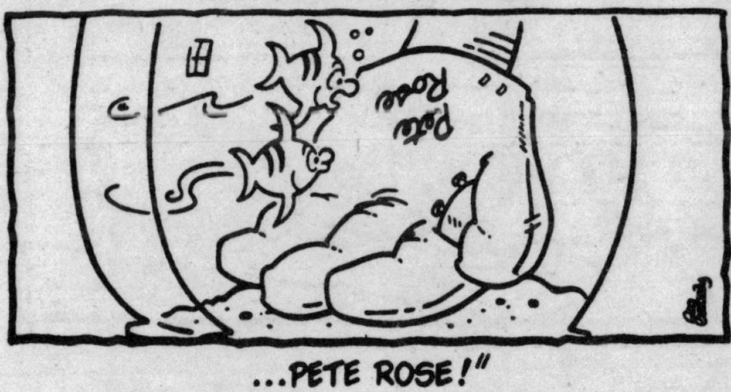
Pete Rose

...PETE ROSE!"

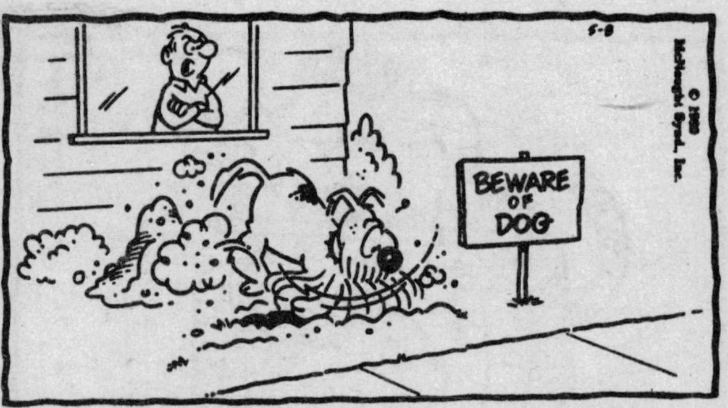
BEWARE OF DOG

"I WISH HE WOULDN'T DIG UP THAT FRONT YARD!"

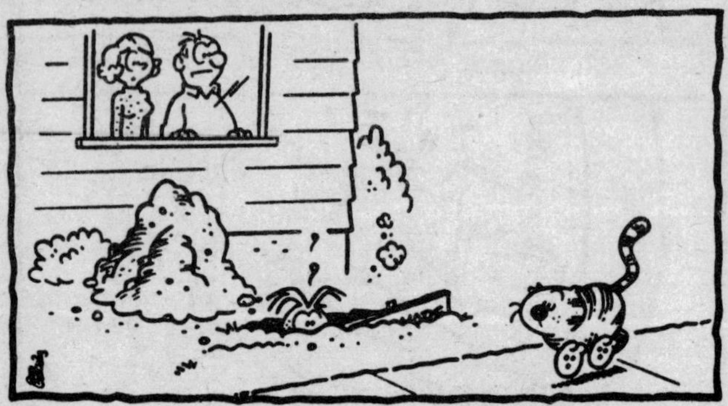

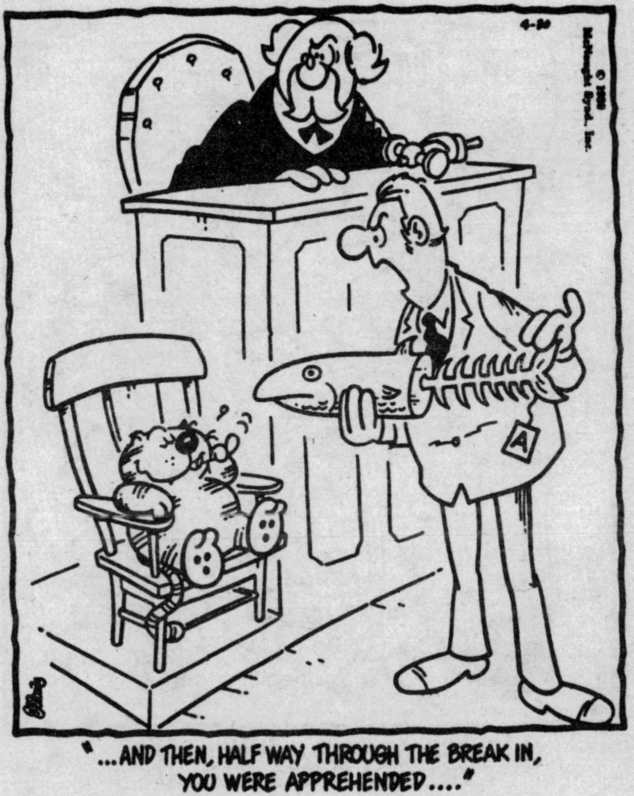

"...AND THEN, HALF WAY THROUGH THE BREAK IN, YOU WERE APPREHENDED...."

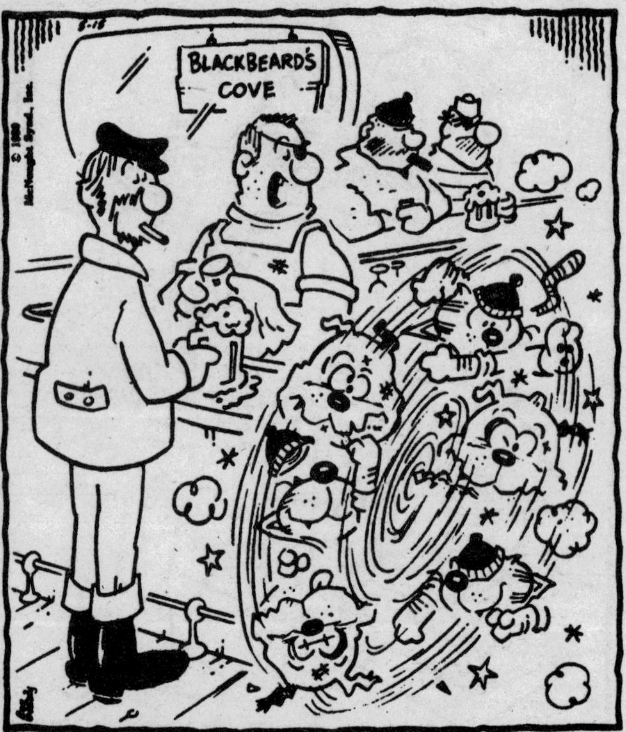
BLACKBEARD'S
COVE

"THERE'S ALWAYS A BRAWL WHEN THE TUNA FLEET'S IN TOWN!"

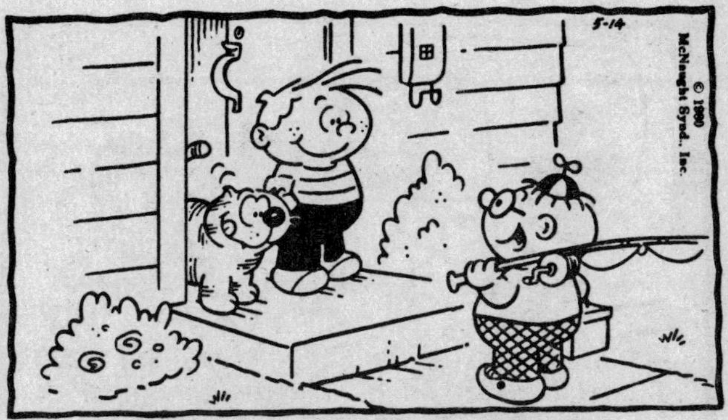
5-14
© 1990 McNaught Synd., Inc.

"THEY STOCKED THE LAKE WITH TROUT!... IT'LL BE LIKE SHOOTING FISH IN A BARREL!"

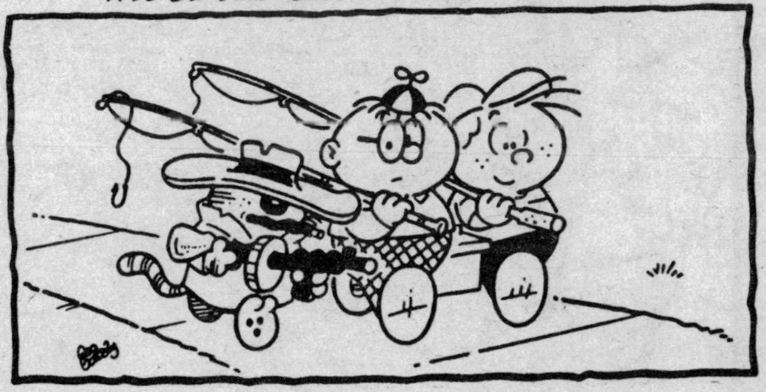

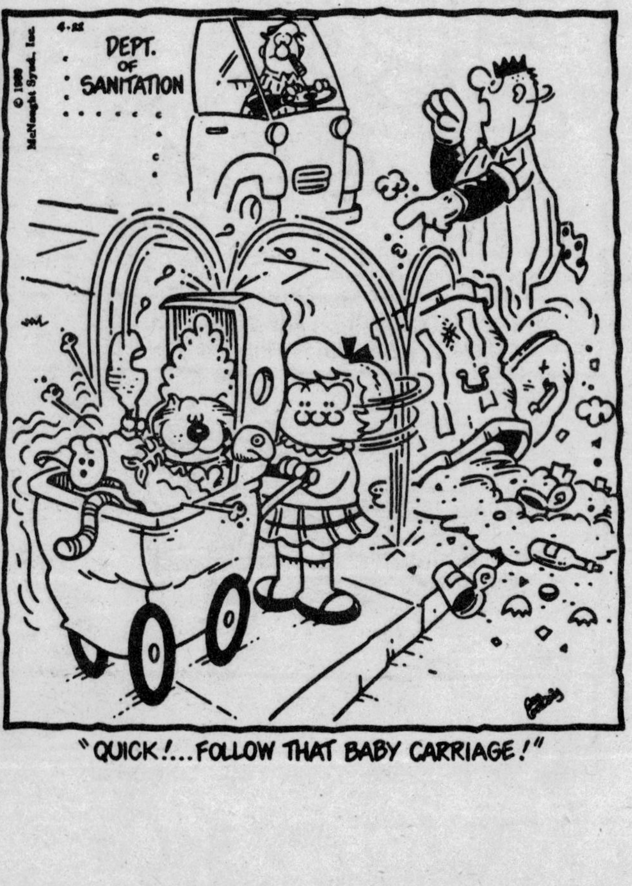
4-22
DEPT. OF SANITATION

"QUICK!... FOLLOW THAT BABY CARRIAGE!"

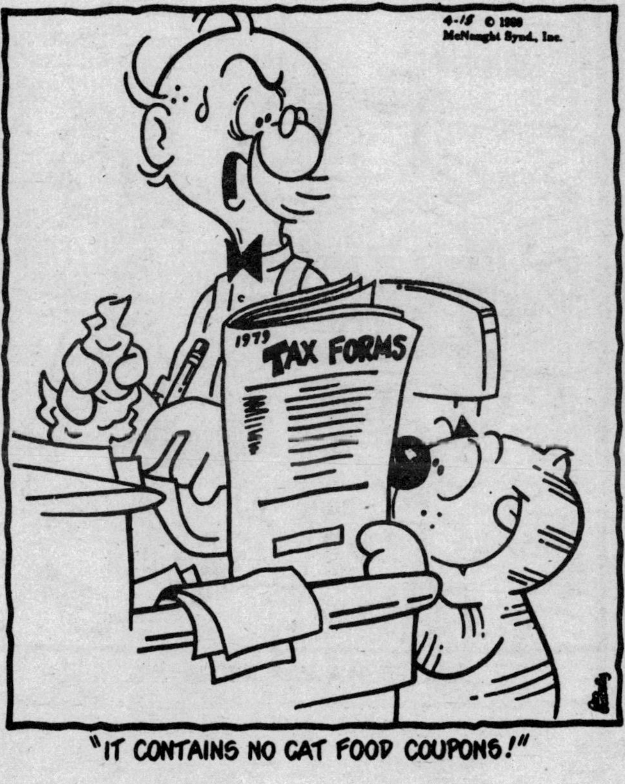
4-15
McNaught Synd., Inc.
1979
TAX FORMS

"IT CONTAINS NO CAT FOOD COUPONS!"

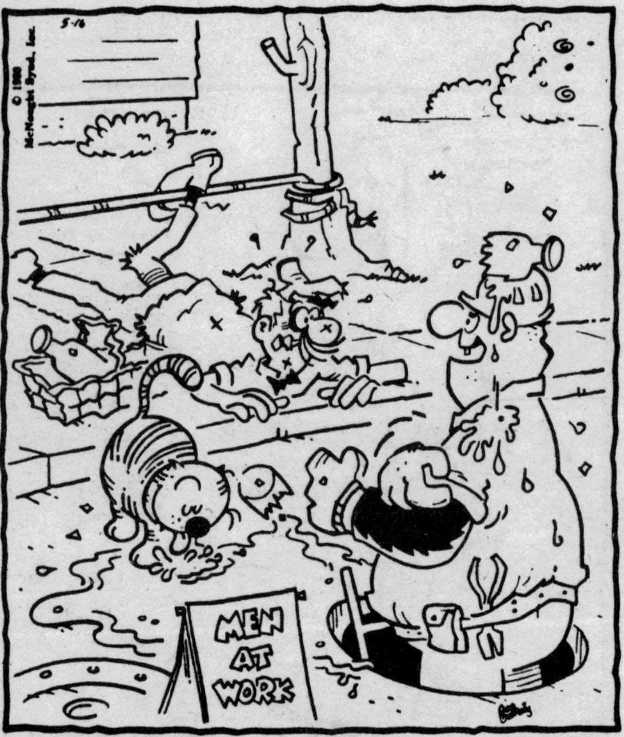
5-16
© 1980 McNaught Synd., Inc.
MEN AT WORK

" DID YOUSE DROP A MILK BOTTLE, PAL ?!... "

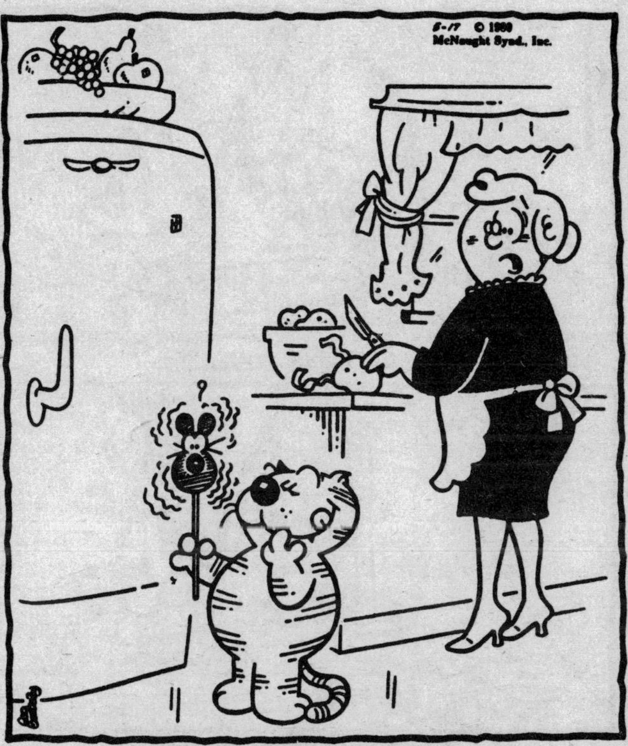
5-17 © 1980
McNaught Synd., Inc.

"I WISH YOU'D STOP EXPERIMENTING WITH THOSE MOUSESICLES!"

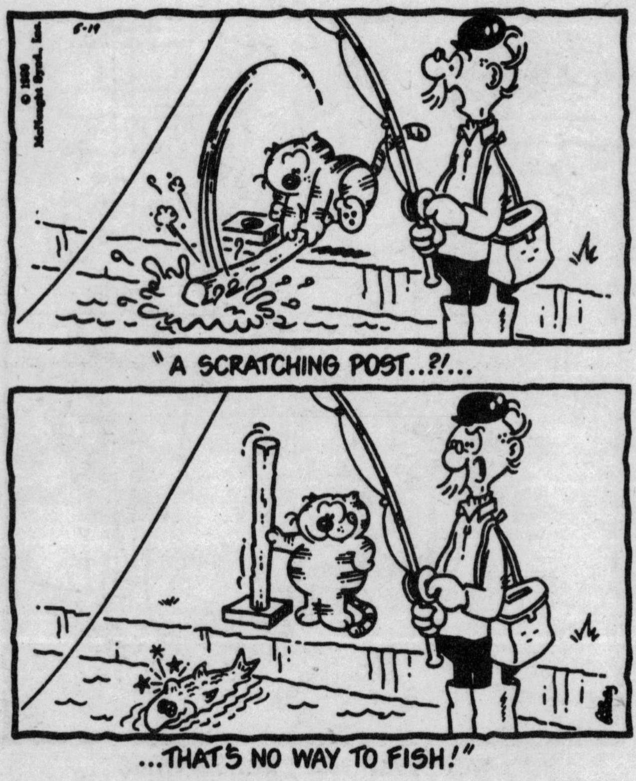
"A SCRATCHING POST..?!...
...THAT'S NO WAY TO FISH!"

6-21
McNaught Synd., Inc.
PHOOT!

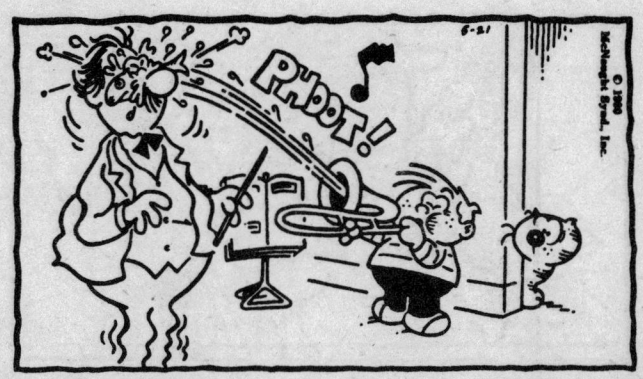

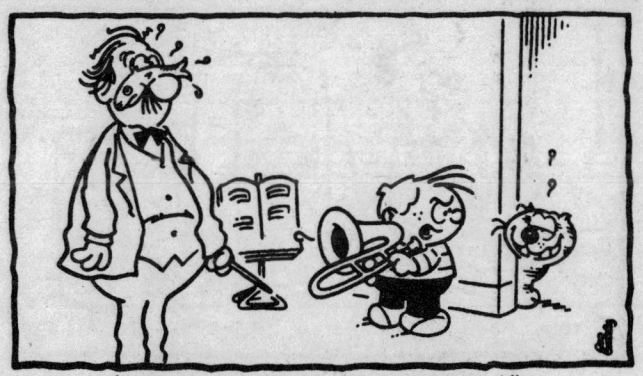

"SORRY ABOUT THAT, PROFESSOR!"

MEOWOWOWOW
4-21
McNaught Synd., Inc.

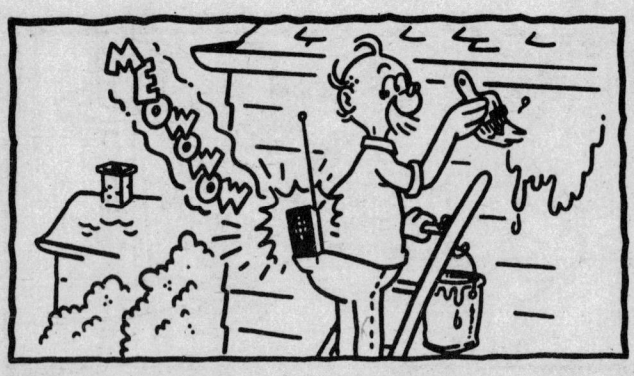

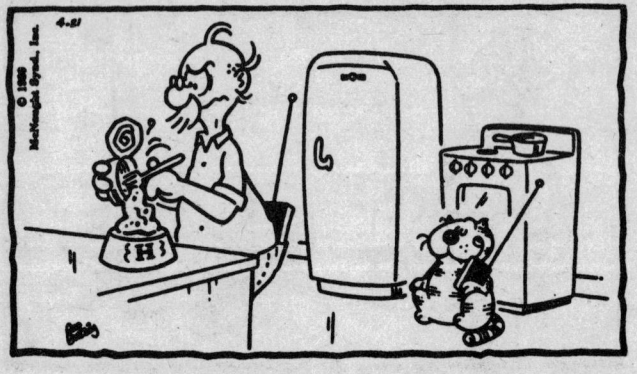

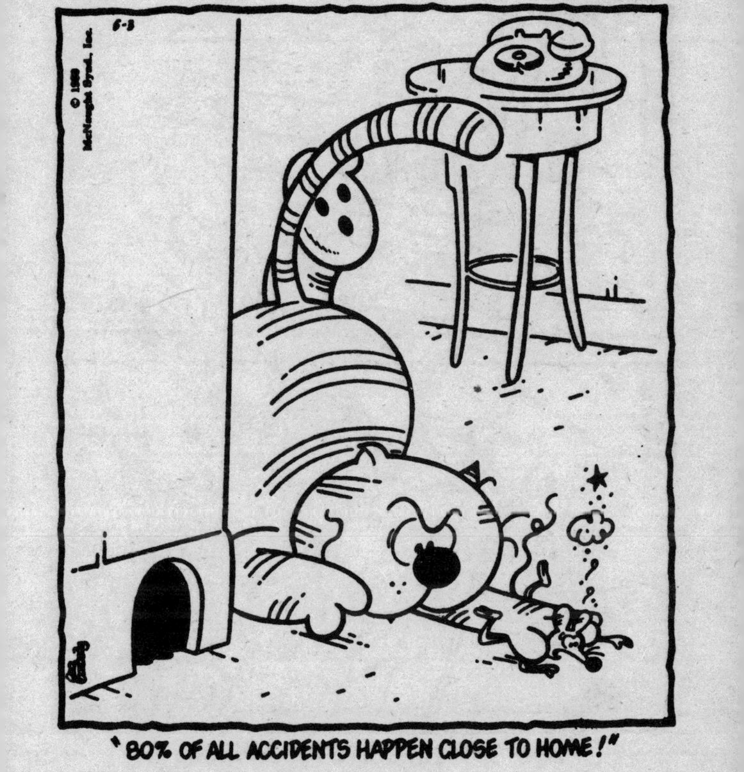
6-3
McNaught Synd., Inc.

"80% OF ALL ACCIDENTS HAPPEN CLOSE TO HOME!"

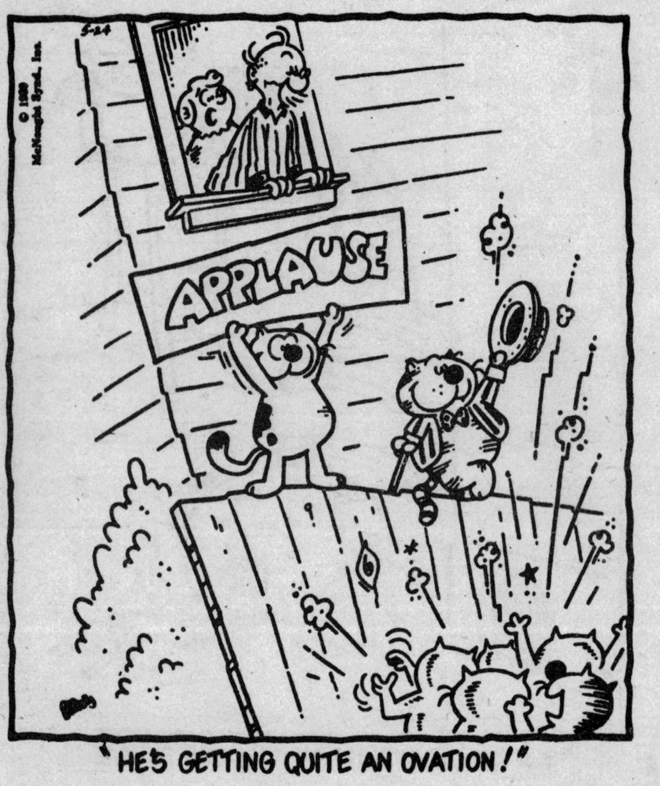
5-24
APPLAUSE

"HE'S GETTING QUITE AN OVATION!"

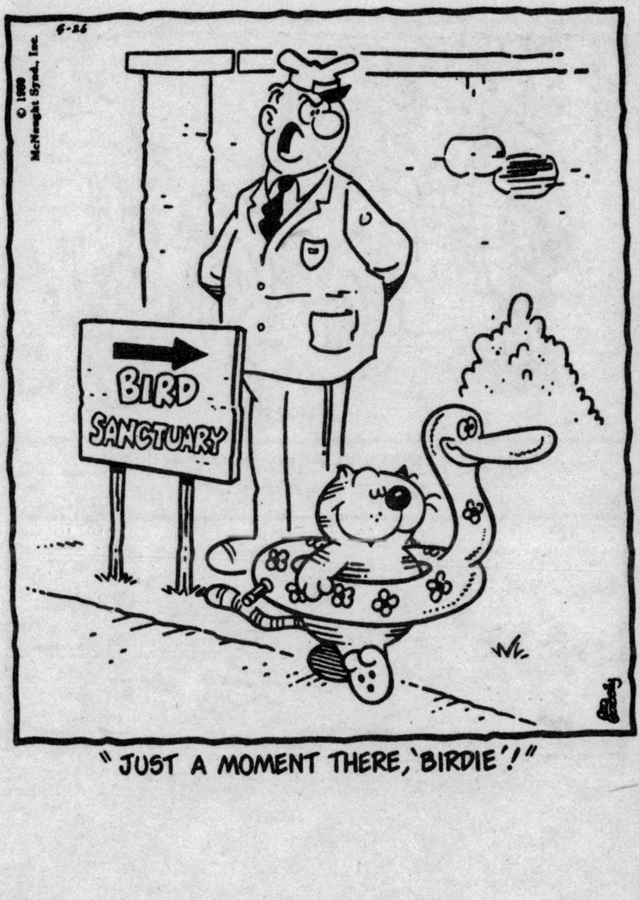
BIRD
SANCTUARY

"JUST A MOMENT THERE, 'BIRDIE'!"

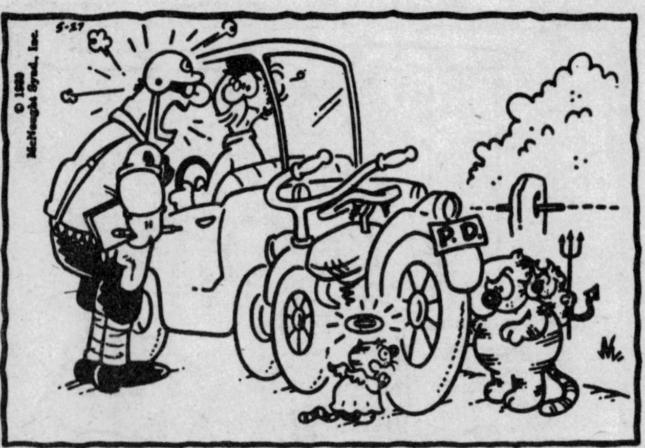
5-27
McNaught Synd., Inc.
P.D.

"OH, NO, HEATHCLIFF!... DON'T LET THE AIR OUT OF HIS TIRES!"

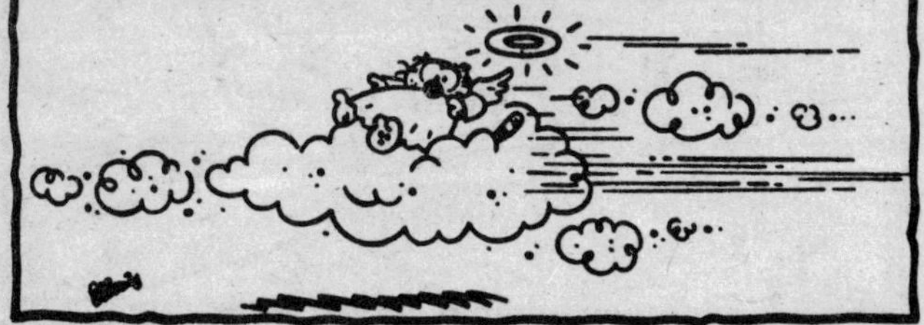

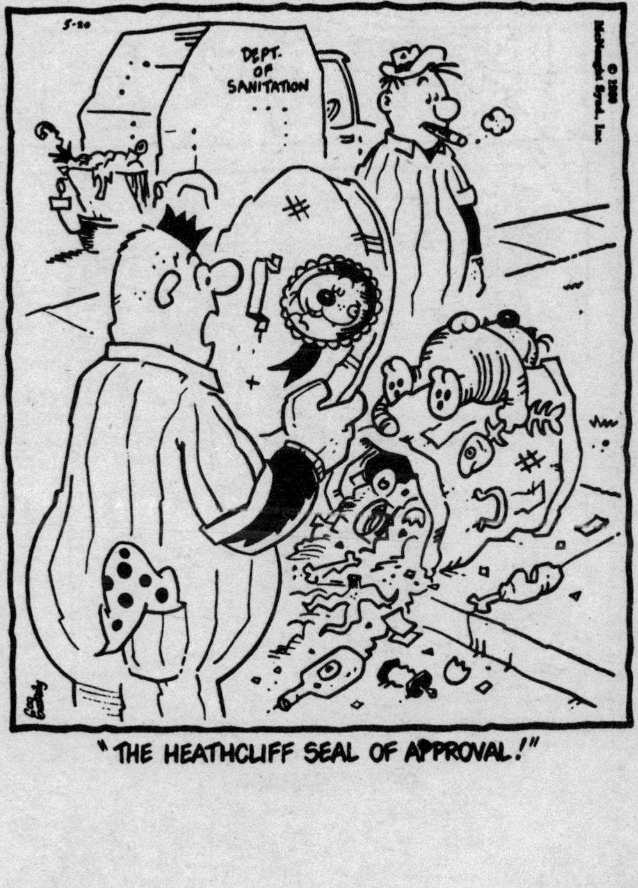
5-20
DEPT. OF SANITATION

"THE HEATHCLIFF SEAL OF APPROVAL!"

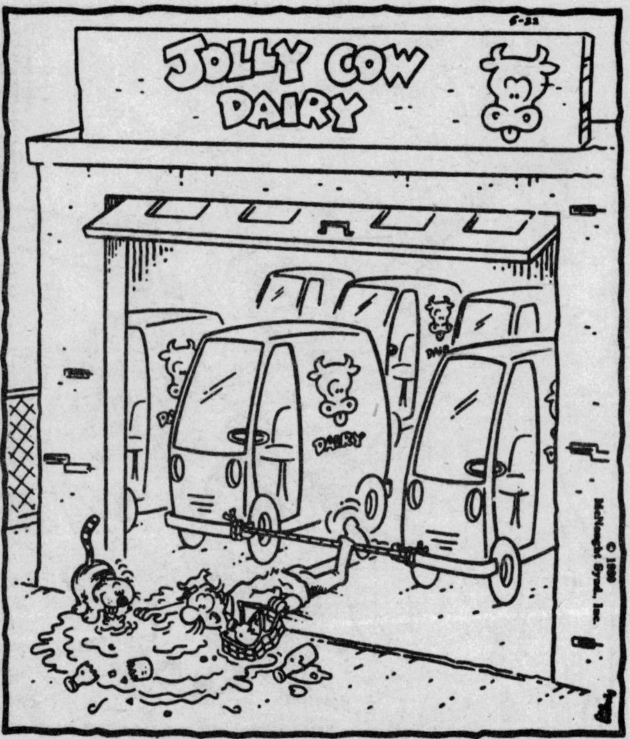
6-22
JOLLY COW DAIRY
DAIRY
McNaught Synd., Inc.

"YOU COULD AT LEAST LET ME GET OUT OF THE GARAGE!"

"WERE YOU AFTER THIS CLOCK AGAIN?!"

"WHAT'S A COCKOO DOING IN THE BIRD BATH?!"

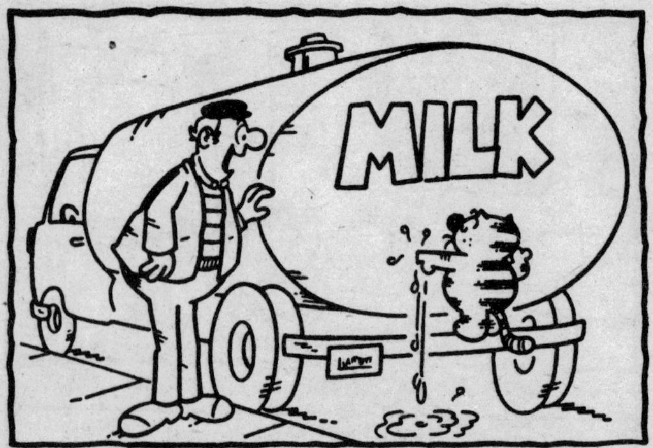
MILK

"THERE'S A BIG REWARD IN THIS FOR YOU, FELLA!"

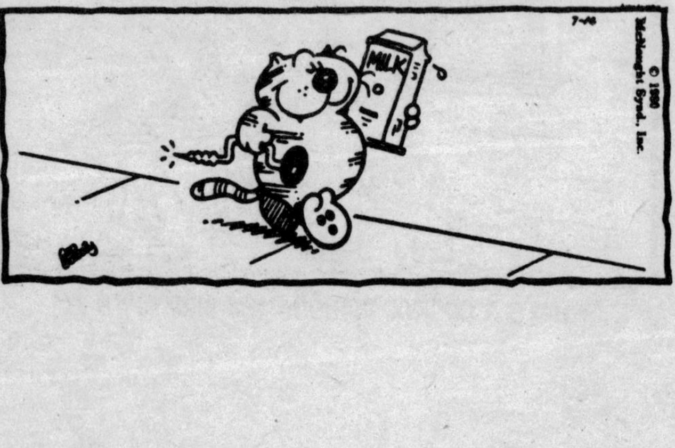
MILK
© 1980 McNaught Synd., Inc.

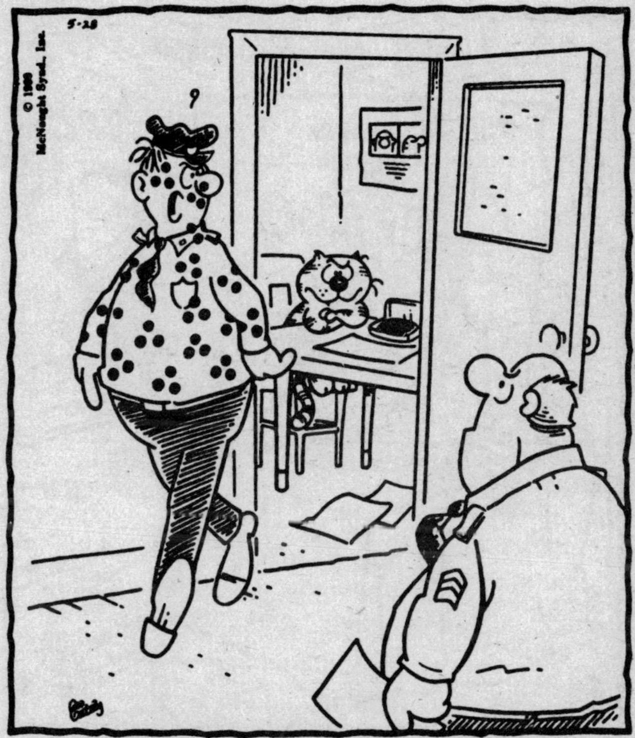
5-28
McNaught Synd., Inc.

"FINGERPRINT HIM YOURSELF, SARGE!"

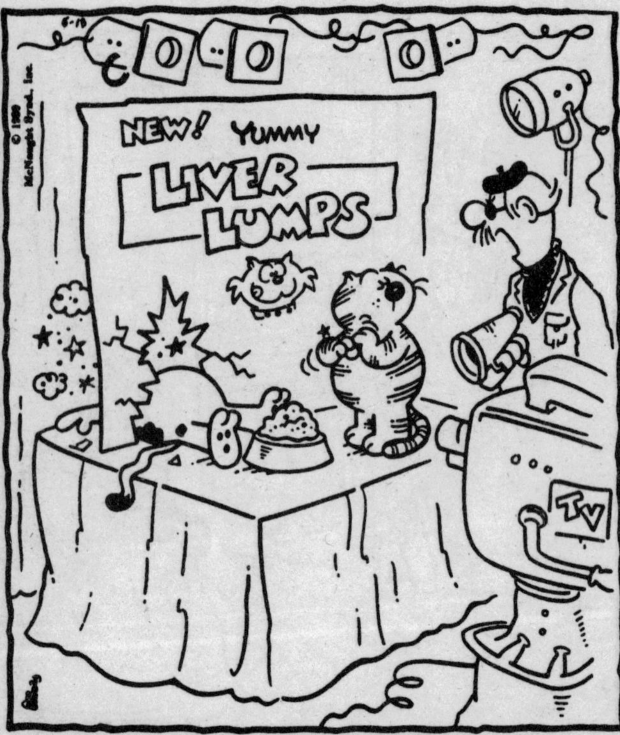
6-18
© 1988 McNaught Synd. Inc.
NEW! YUMMY
LIVER LUMPS
TV

"YOU'RE SUPPOSED TO JUST *NUDGE* HIM AWAY FROM THE DISH!"

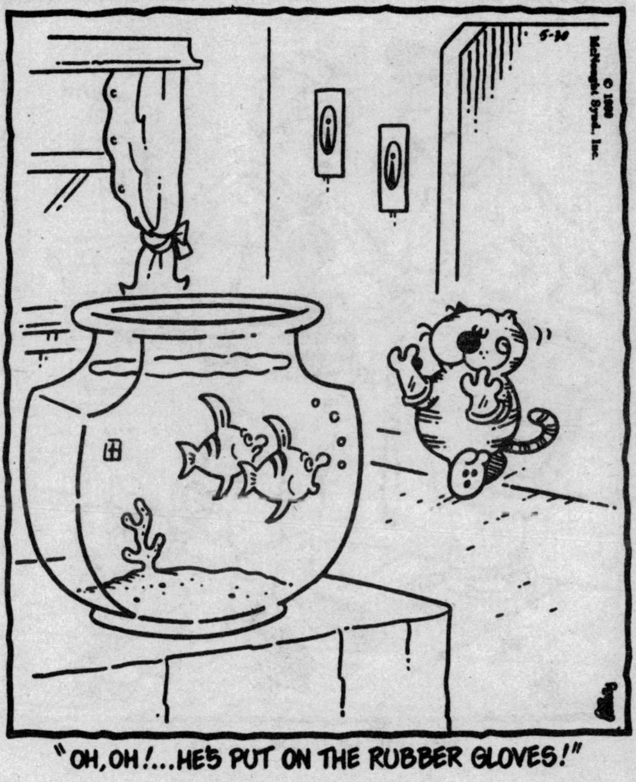

"OH, OH!...HE'S PUT ON THE RUBBER GLOVES!"

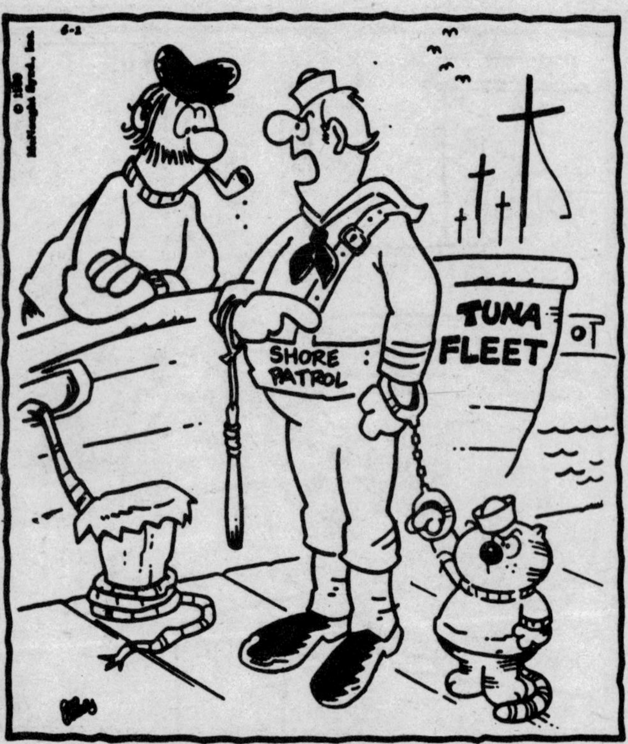
TUNA
FLEET
SHORE
PATROL

"THIS ONE OF YOUR CREW ?!"

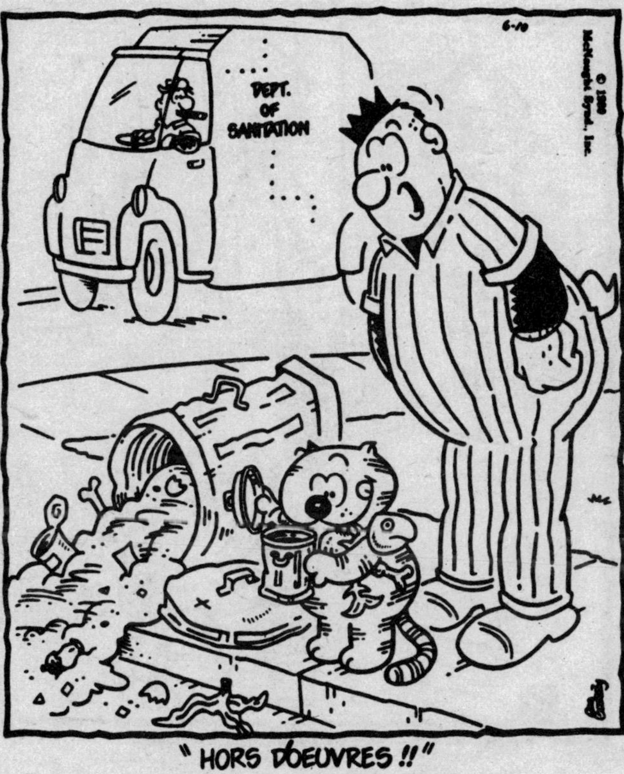
6-10
DEPT. OF SANITATION

"HORS D'OEUVRES!!"

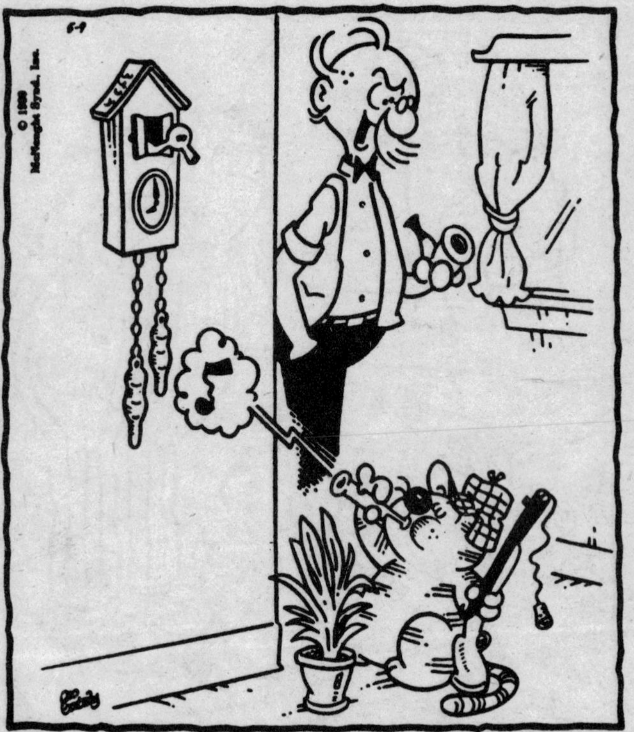
6-9
McNaught Synd., Inc.

"CAN I SEE YOUR HUNTING LICENSE ?!"

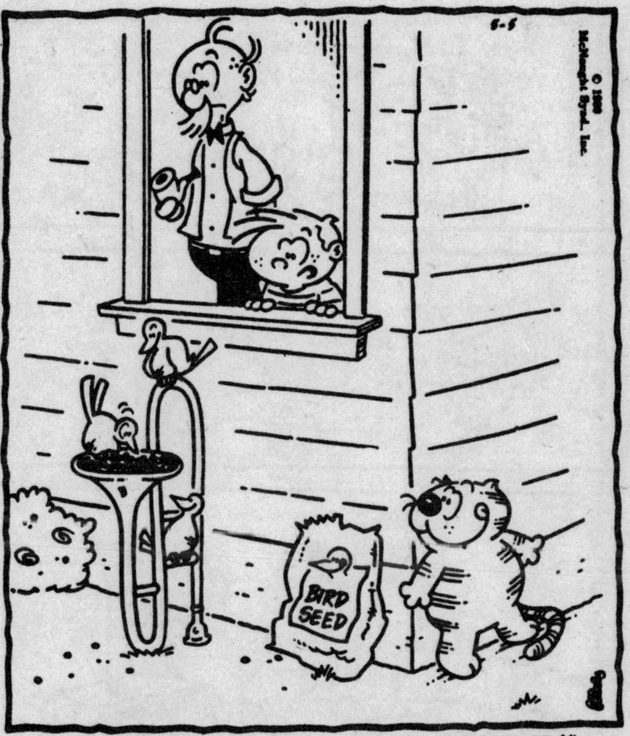
BIRD SEED

"HE'S USING MY TROMBONE FOR A BIRD FEEDER!"

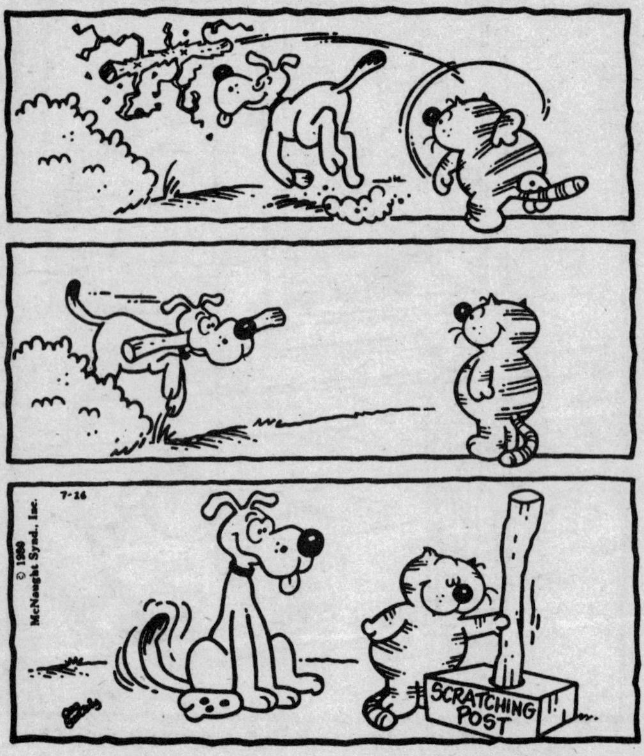
7-26
McNaught Synd., Inc.
SCRATCHING POST

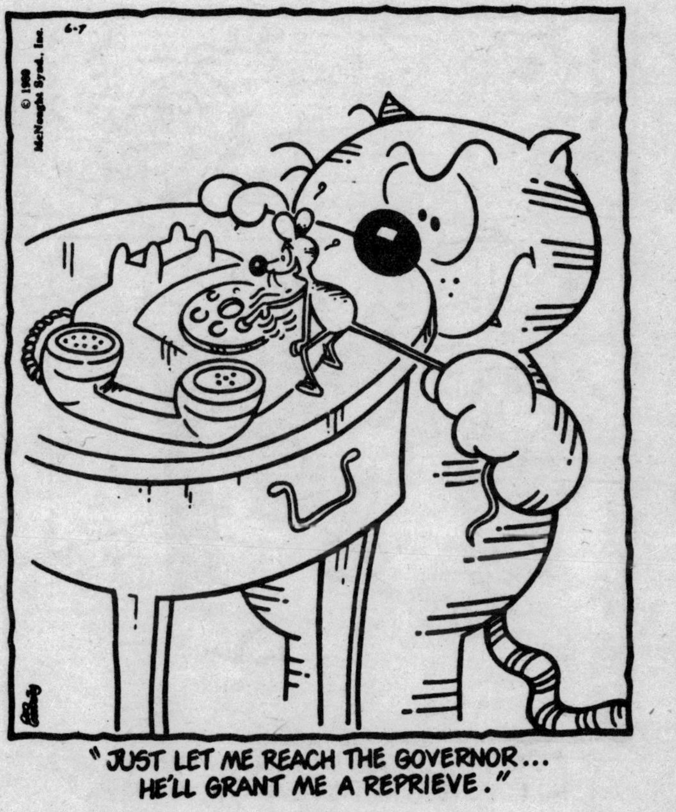
6-7
© 1980 McNaught Synd., Inc.

"JUST LET ME REACH THE GOVERNOR...
HE'LL GRANT ME A REPRIEVE."

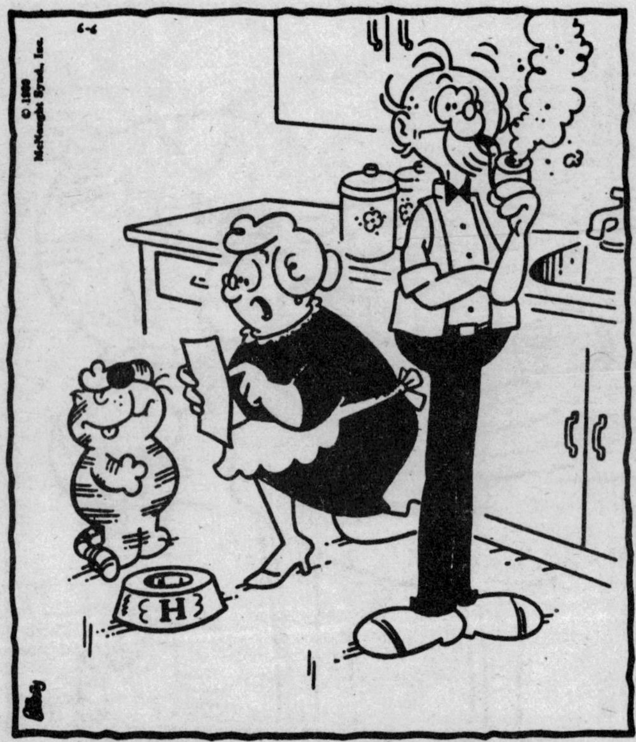
McNaught Synd., Inc.
6-6
H

"THE VET PUT YOU ON A BLAND DIET....
NO LOBSTER, NO PHEASANT, NO SHRIMP..."

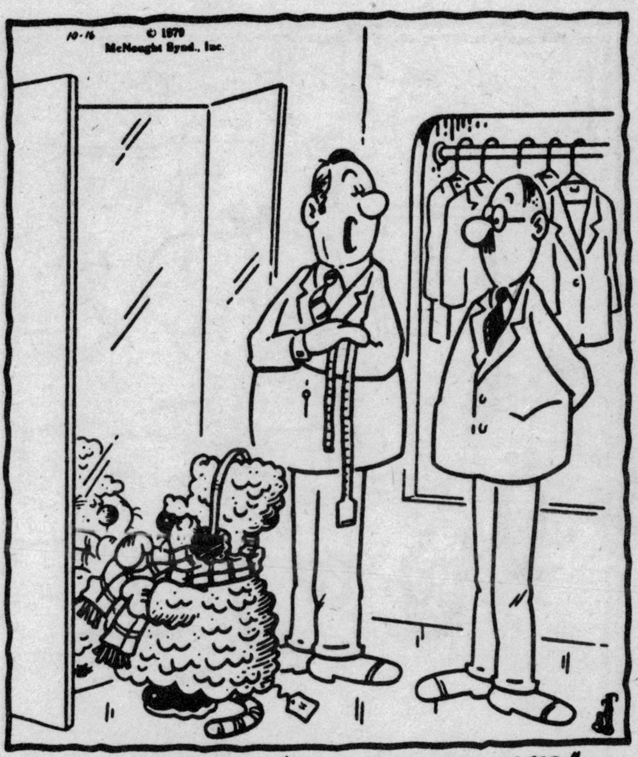
10-16 © 1979
McNaught Synd., Inc.

"IT'S A SURE SIGN WE'RE IN FOR A COLD WINTER."

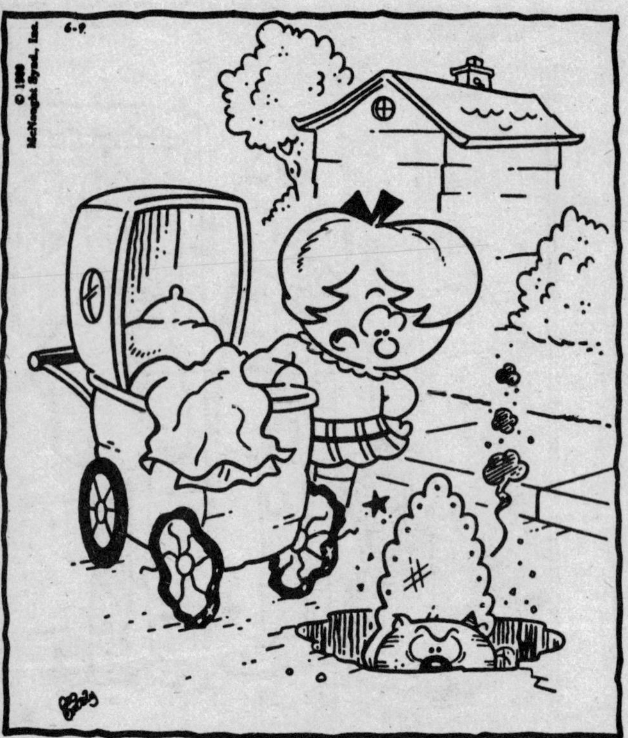
© 1986 McNaught Synd., Inc.
6-9

"I WISH THEY'D DO SOMETHING ABOUT THESE POT HOLES!"

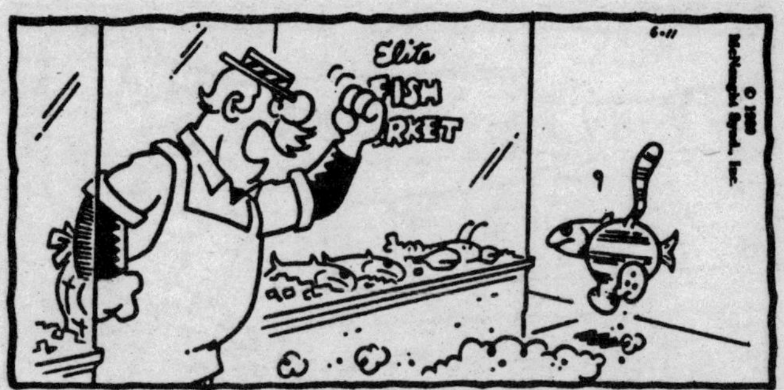
Elite
6-11

"HEATHCLIFF, YOU'RE A THIEVING SCOUNDREL!"

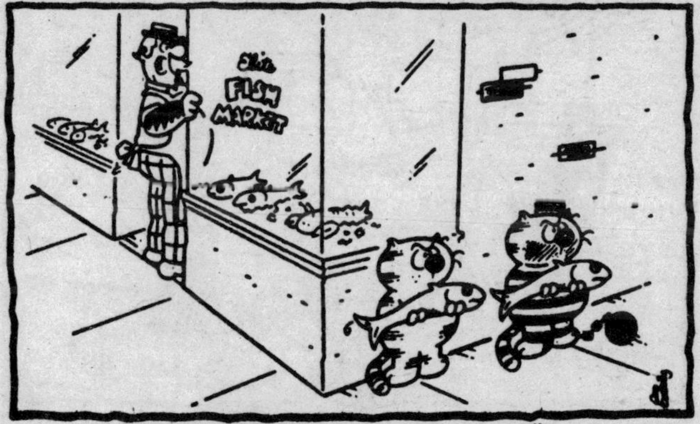
Elite
FISH
MARKET

"....AND, SO'S YOUR OLD MAN!"

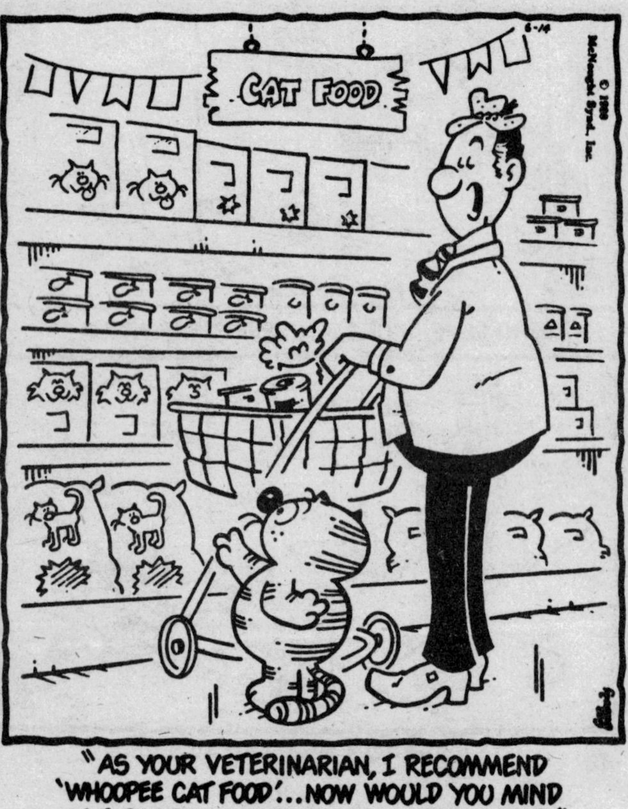
CAT FOOD
6-14
© 1988 McNaught Synd., Inc.

"AS YOUR VETERINARIAN, I RECOMMEND 'WHOOPEE CAT FOOD'...NOW WOULD YOU MIND IF I CONTINUE WITH MY OWN SHOPPING?"

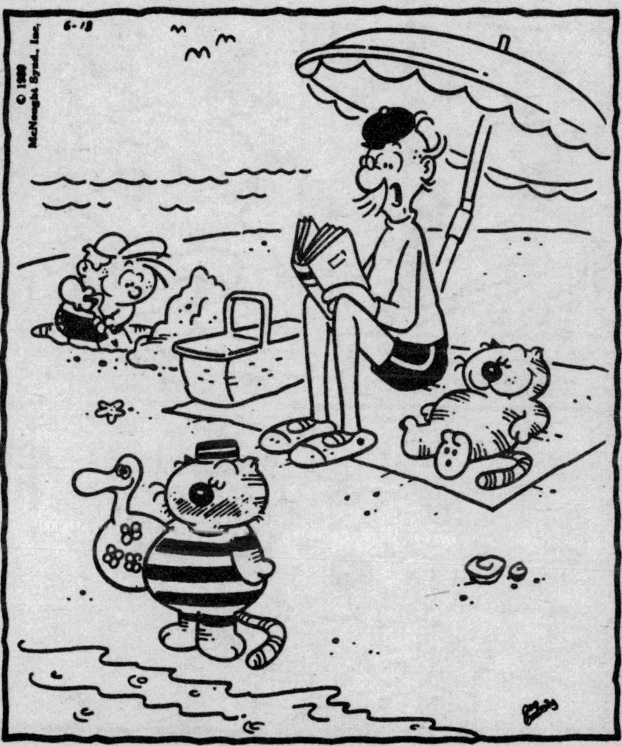
6-18
McNaught Synd., Inc.

"I SEE YOUR DAD IS WEARING HIS CUT OFFS."

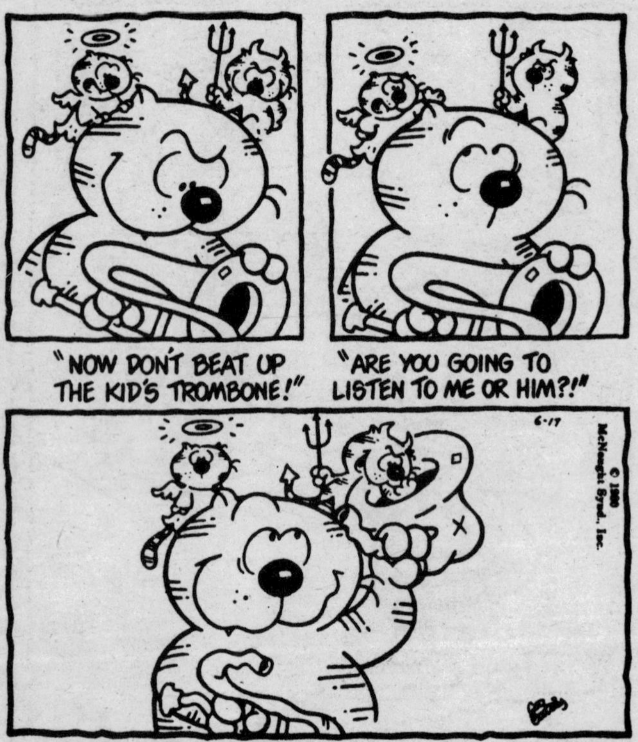
6-17
© 1980 McNaught Synd., Inc.

"NOW DON'T BEAT UP THE KID'S TROMBONE!"

"ARE YOU GOING TO LISTEN TO ME OR HIM?!"

"'ATTA BOY!"

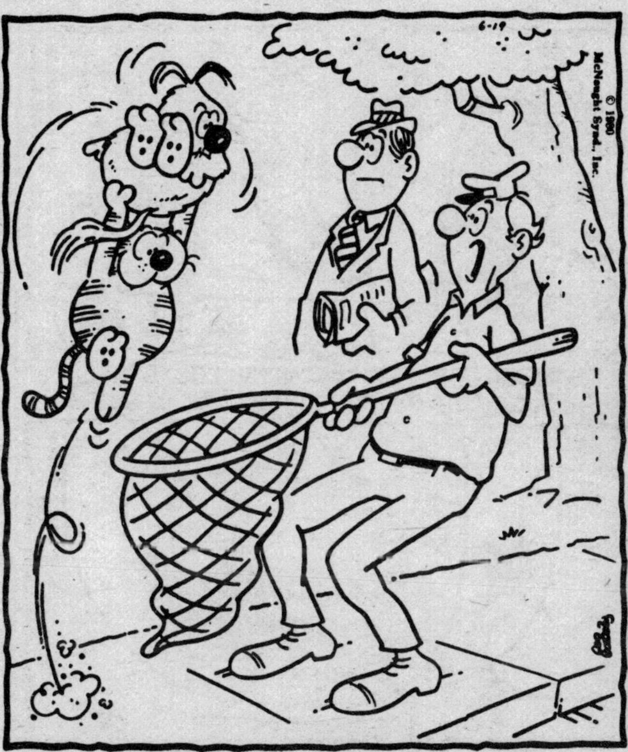
6-19
© 1980 McNaught Synd., Inc.

"HE'S PRACTICING HIS SLAM DUNK!"

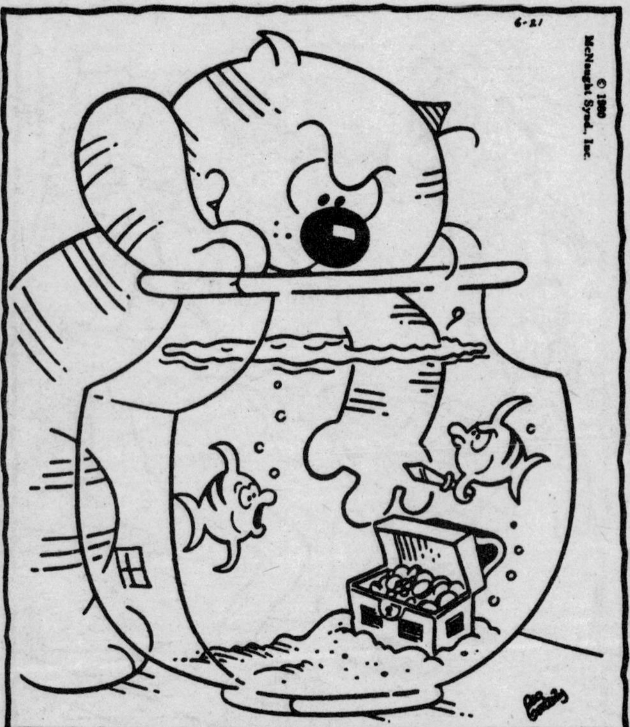
6-21
© 1980 McNaught Synd., Inc.

"FOR CRYING OUT LOUD!... LET HIM HAVE THE TREASURE!"

6-20
McNaught Synd., Inc.

"HEATHCLIFF!...SUPPER!"

"I WISH YOU WOULDN'T COME DOWN THE CHIMNEY!"

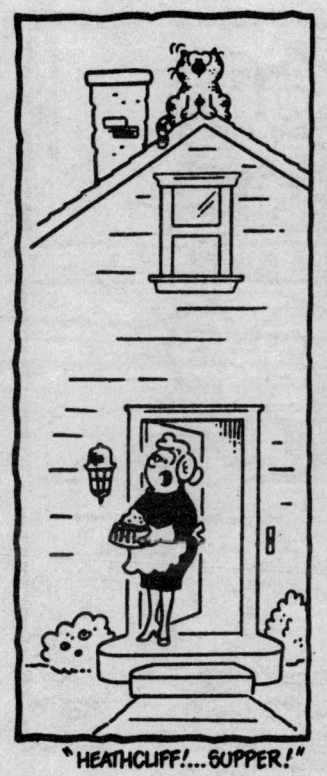

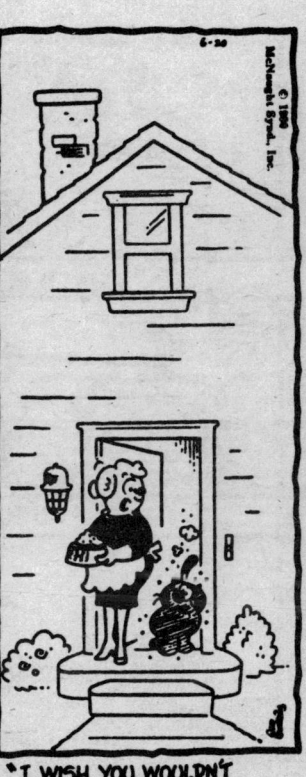

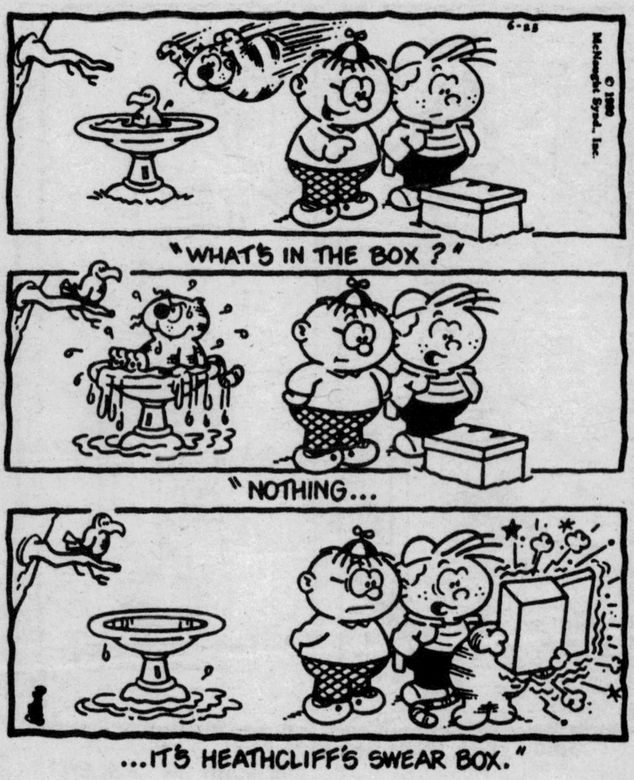
6-23
© 1980 McNaught Synd., Inc.
"WHAT'S IN THE BOX ?"
"NOTHING...
...IT'S HEATHCLIFF'S SWEAR BOX."

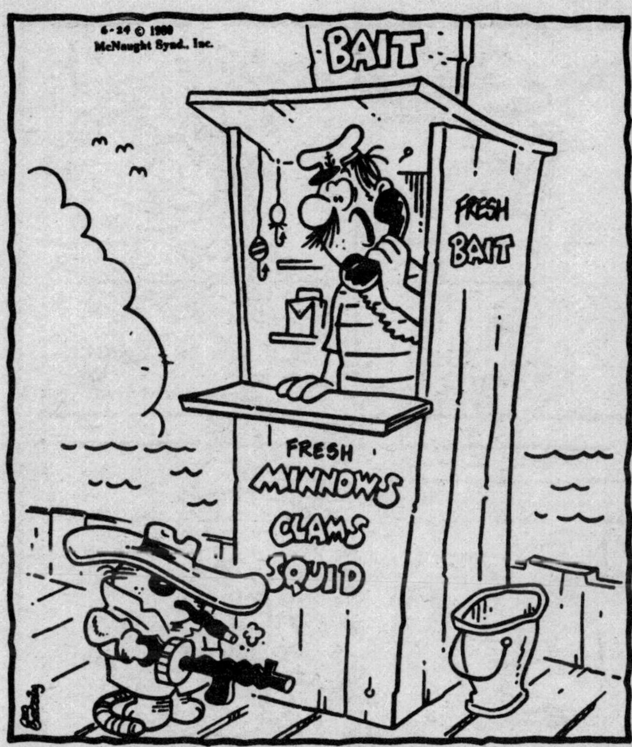
6-24 © 1980
McNaught Synd., Inc.
BAIT
FRESH
BAIT
FRESH
MINNOWS
CLAMS
SQUID

"HELLO ?... HARBOR PATROL...."

6-25
© 1989 McNaught Synd., Inc.

"YOU KILLED A FRISBEE ?!"

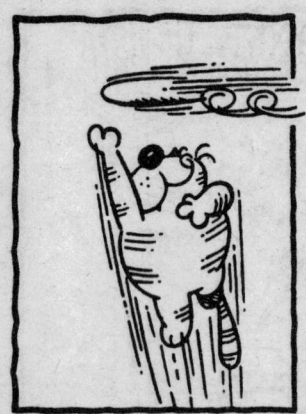

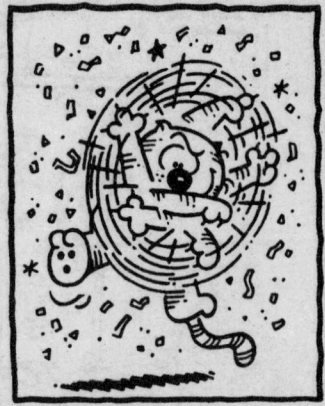

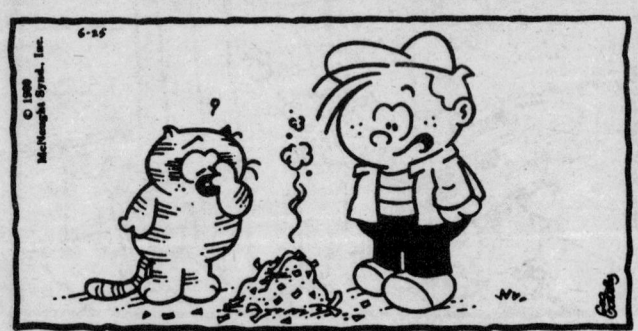

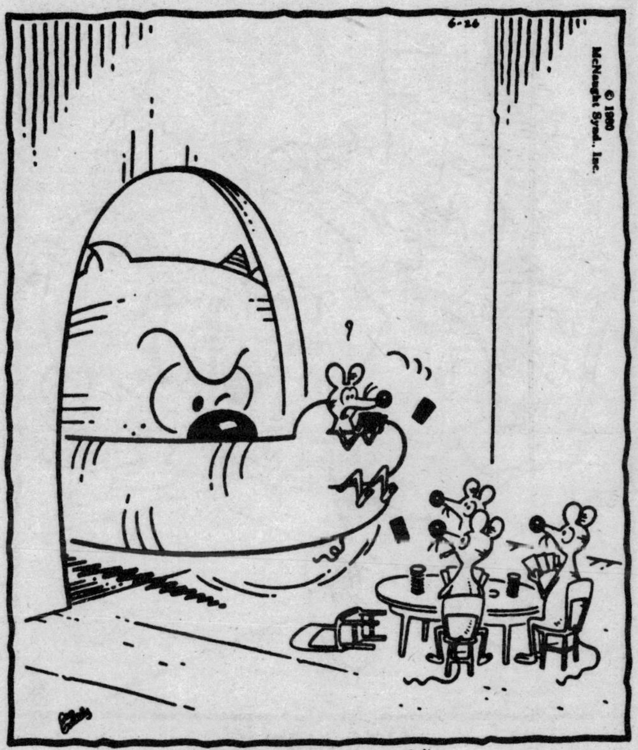
6-26
© 1980 McNaught Synd., Inc.

"DEAL ME OUT!"

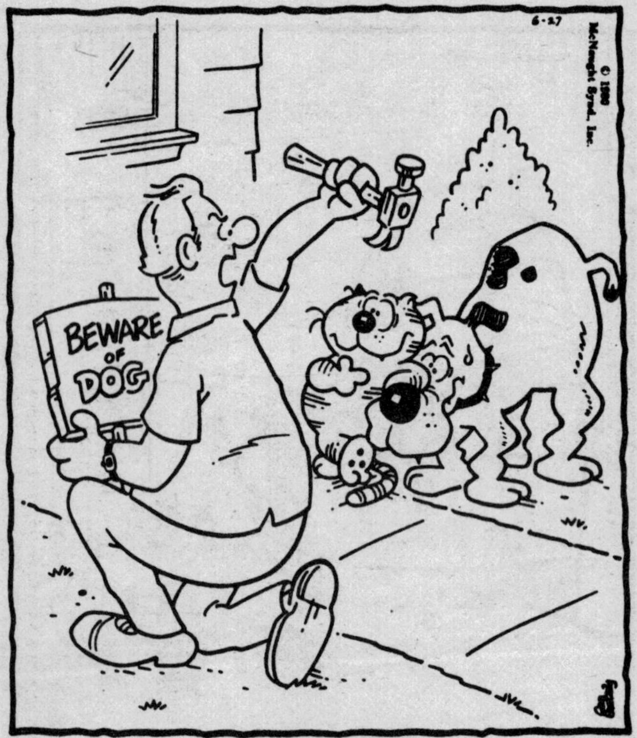
BEWARE OF DOG
6-27
McNaught Synd., Inc.

"YES...HIM!!"

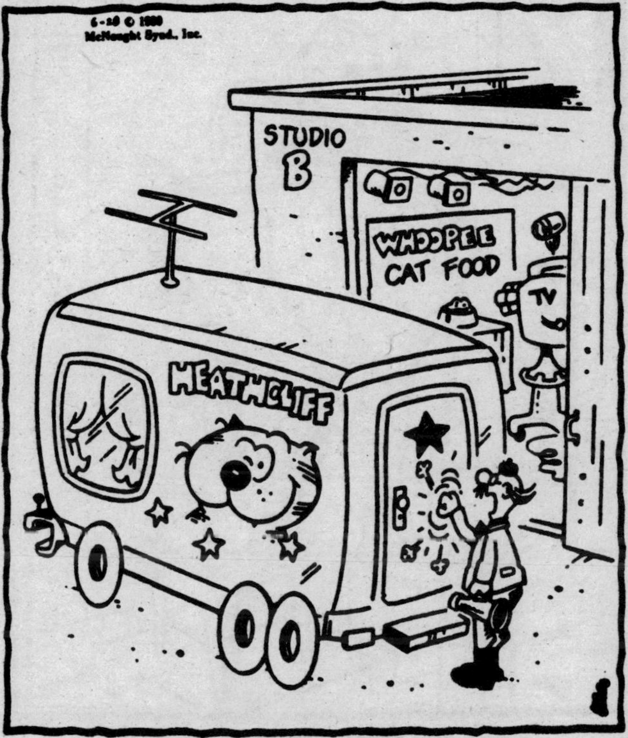
6-28 © 1980
McNaught Synd., Inc.
STUDIO
B
WHOOPEE
CAT FOOD
TV
HEATHCLIFF

"WE'RE READY FOR THE STAR."

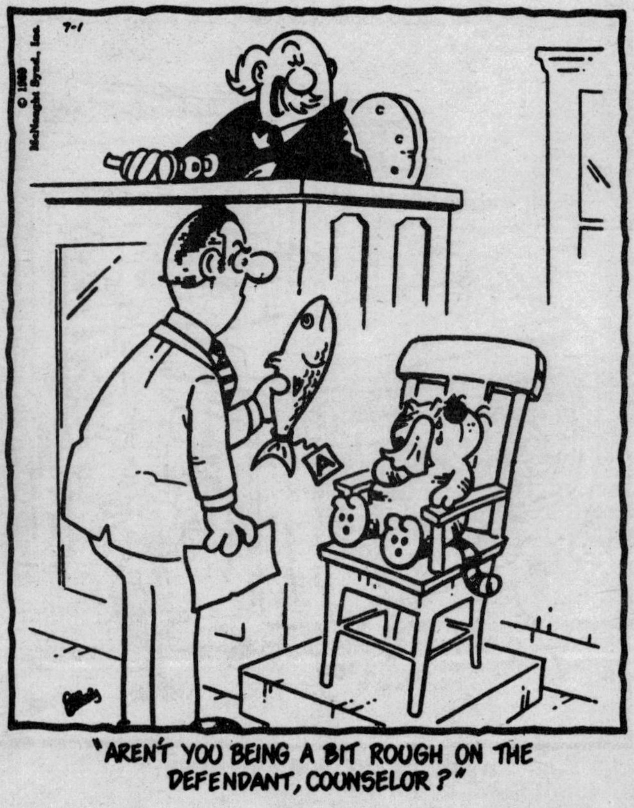
7-1
McNaught Synd., Inc.
A

"AREN'T YOU BEING A BIT ROUGH ON THE DEFENDANT, COUNSELOR?"

10-22
TUNA
FLEET

"DID YE THROW THAT STOWAWAY IN THE BRIG, MATEY?"

"AYE, CAPT'N!"

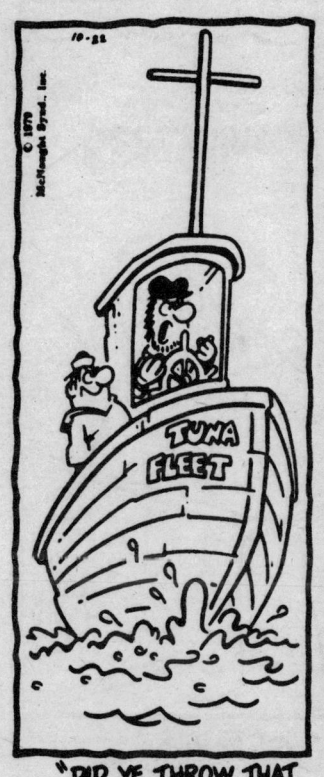

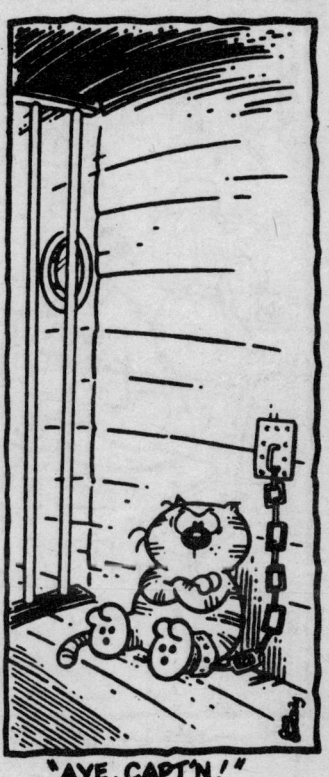

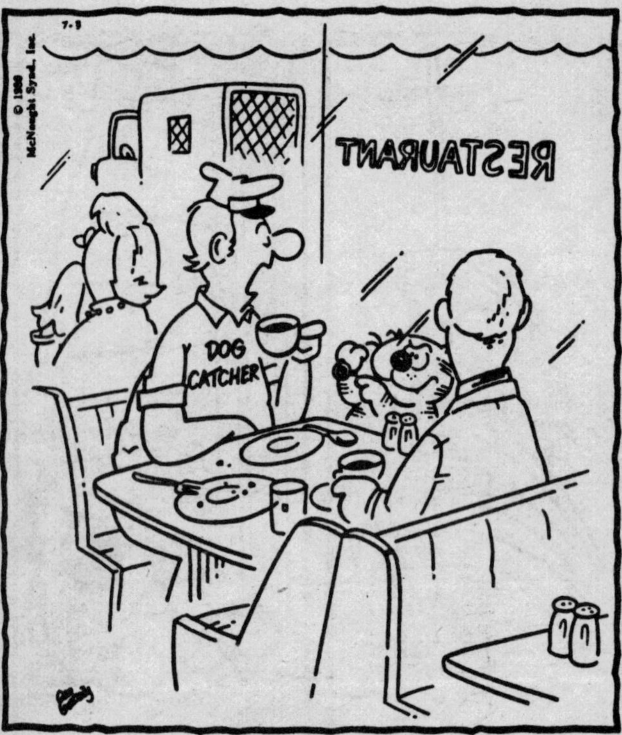
McNaught Synd., Inc.
RESTAURANT
DOG CATCHER

"MY LUNCH HOUR MUST BE OVER."

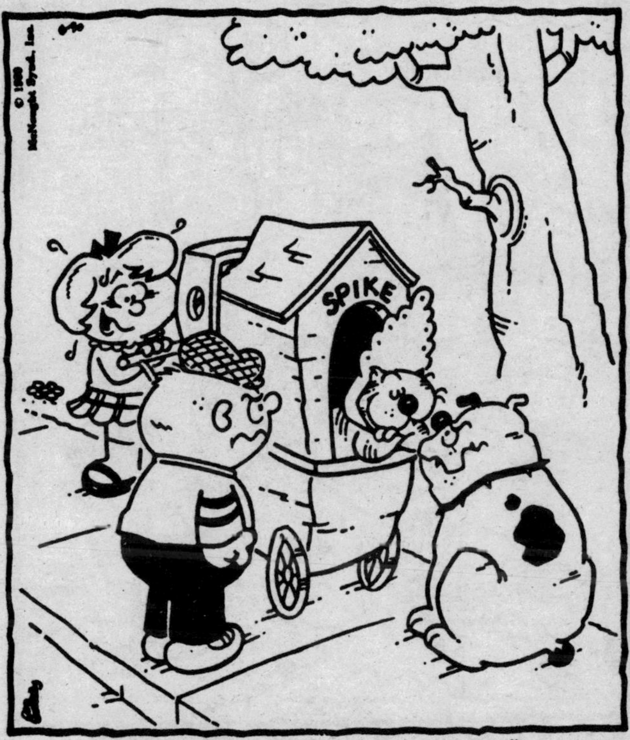
SPIKE

"WE WERE LOOKING AT CAMPERS."

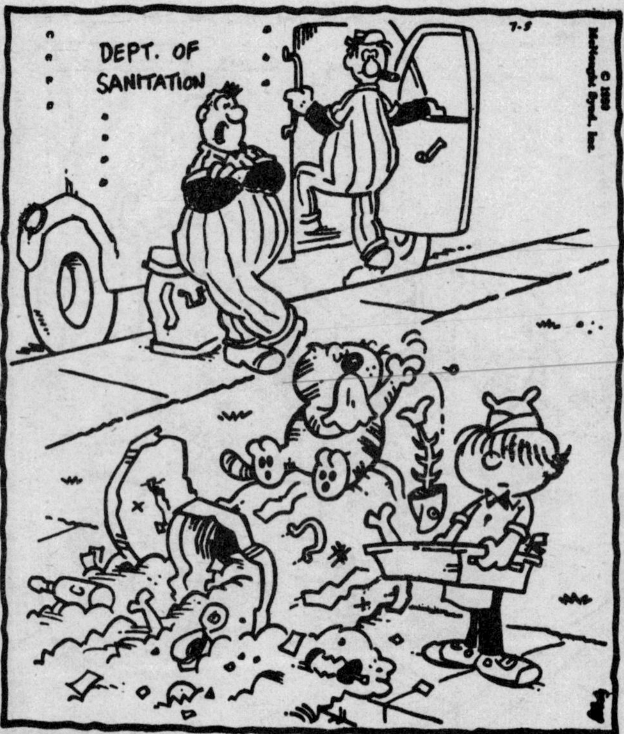
DEPT. OF
SANITATION
7-9

"HE'S A LOT NEATER SINCE HE HIRED A BUS BOY."

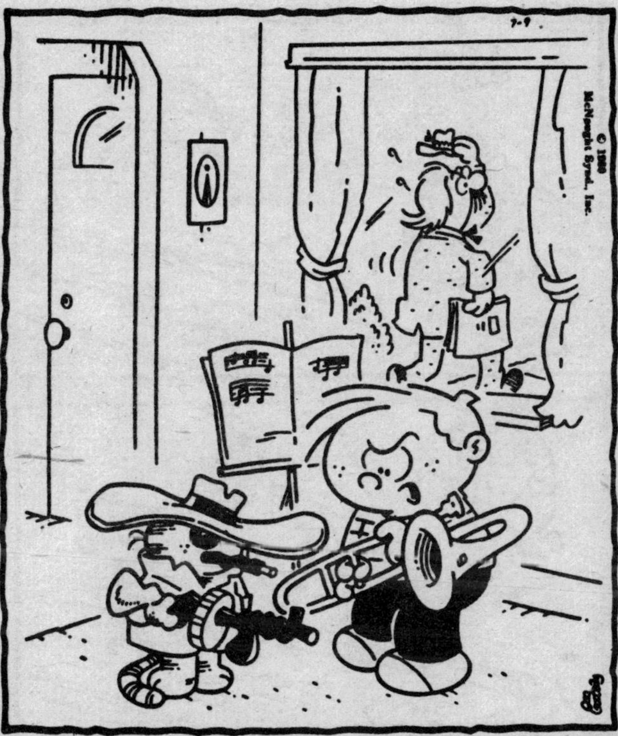
7-9
© 1989 McNaught Synd., Inc.

"DID YOU THREATEN MY MUSIC TEACHER ?!"

7-10
© 1990 McNaught Synd., Inc.
HARRY'S BEEF AND BREW
WET CEMENT
WET CEMENT

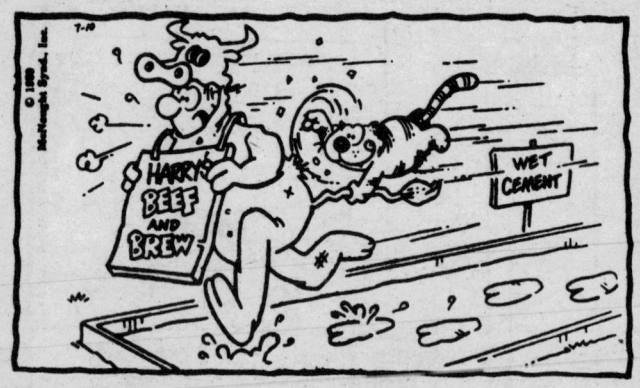

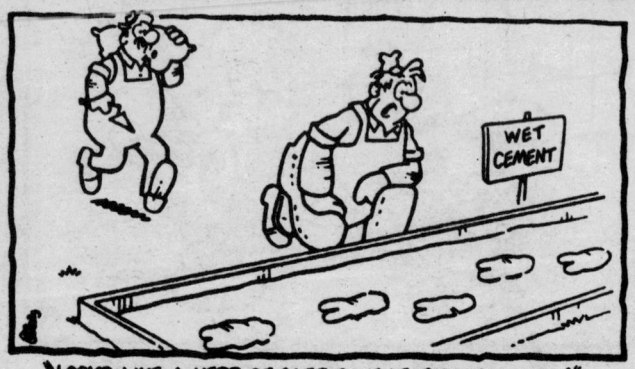

"LOOKS LIKE A HERD OF CATTLE WENT THROUGH HERE!"

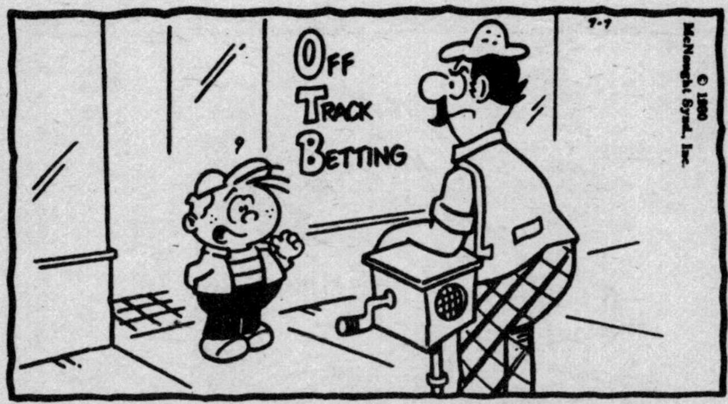
OFF
TRACK
BETTING
9-7
© 1980
McNaught Synd., Inc.

"HEATHCLIFF TOOK HIM INTO THE BETTING PARLOR."

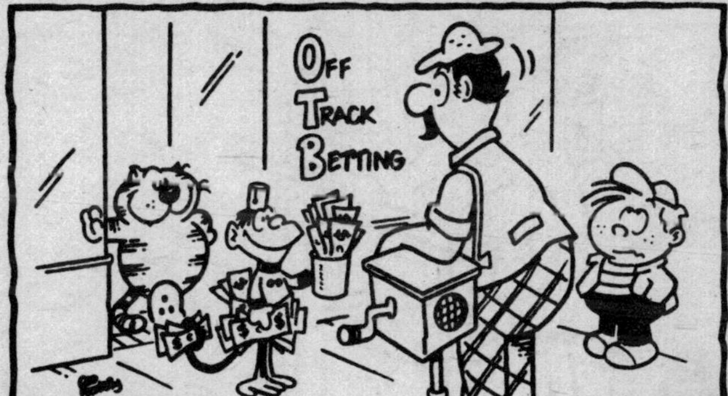
OFF
TRACK
BETTING

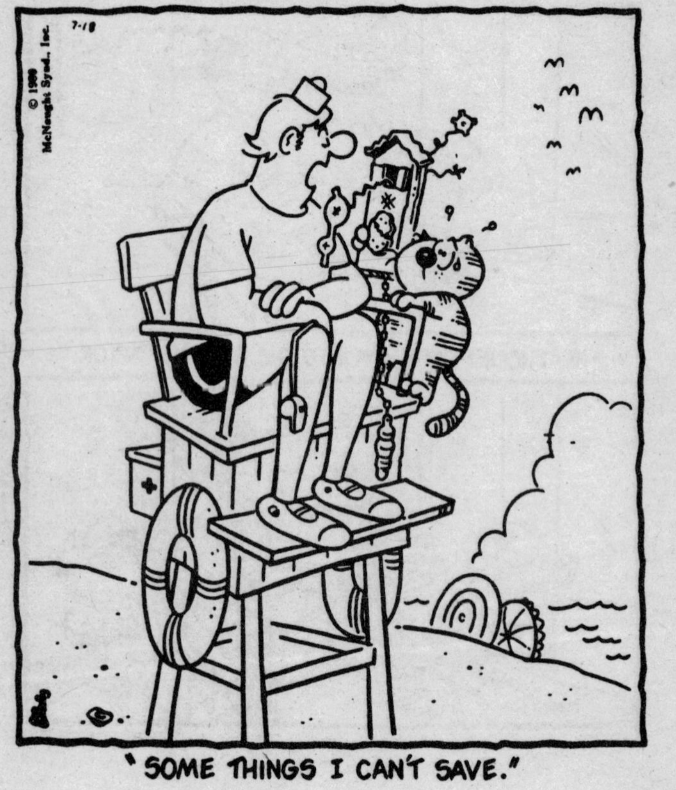
7-18
McNaught Synd., Inc.

"SOME THINGS I CAN'T SAVE."

McNaught Synd., Inc.
7-22
DAIRY
DAIRY

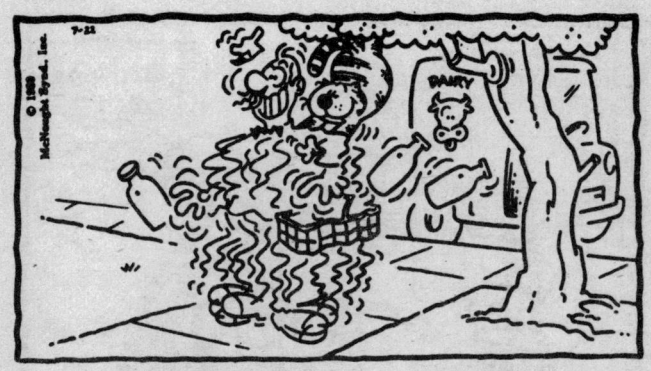

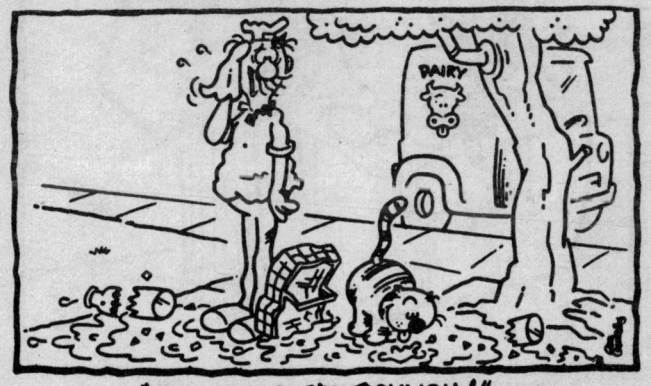

"HE KNOWS I'M TICKLISH!"

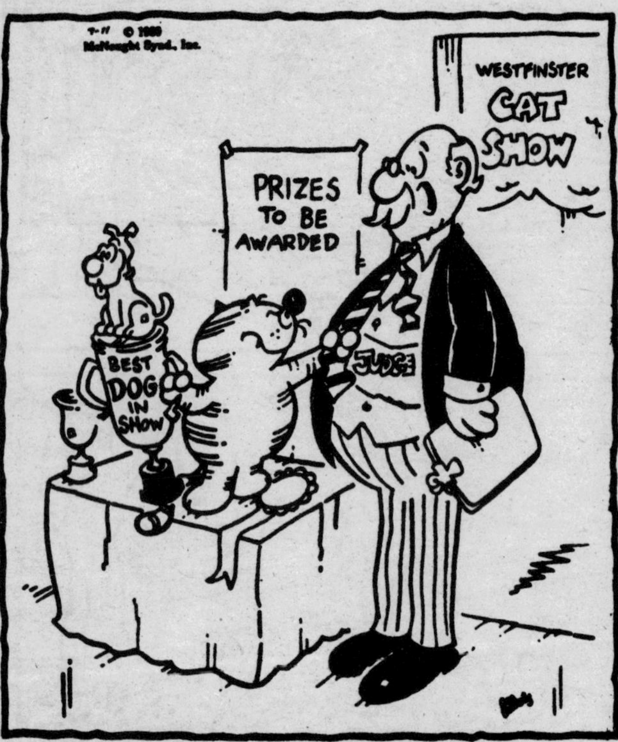
WESTFINSTER
CAT
SHOW
PRIZES
TO BE
AWARDED
BEST
DOG
IN
SHOW
JUDGE

"THERE'S BEEN A SLIGHT ERROR IN SHIPPING..."

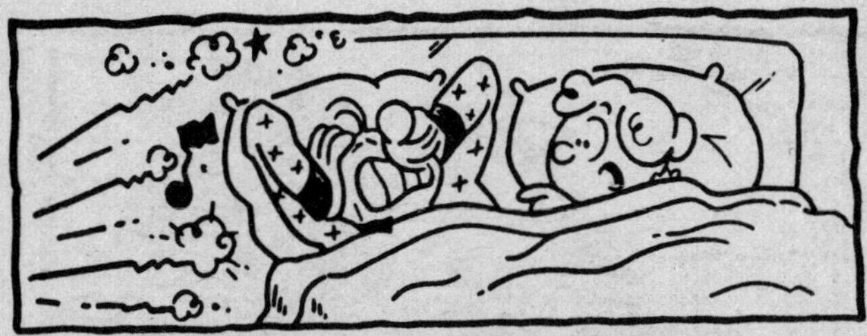

"WHY BLAME HEATHCLIFF ?... IT MIGHT BE ANY CAT IN THE NEIGHBORHOOD."

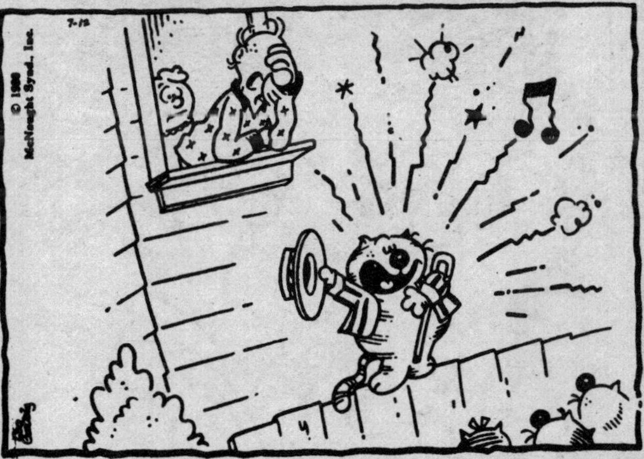
7-12
McNaught Synd., Inc.

"I RECOGNIZE HIS THEME SONG!"

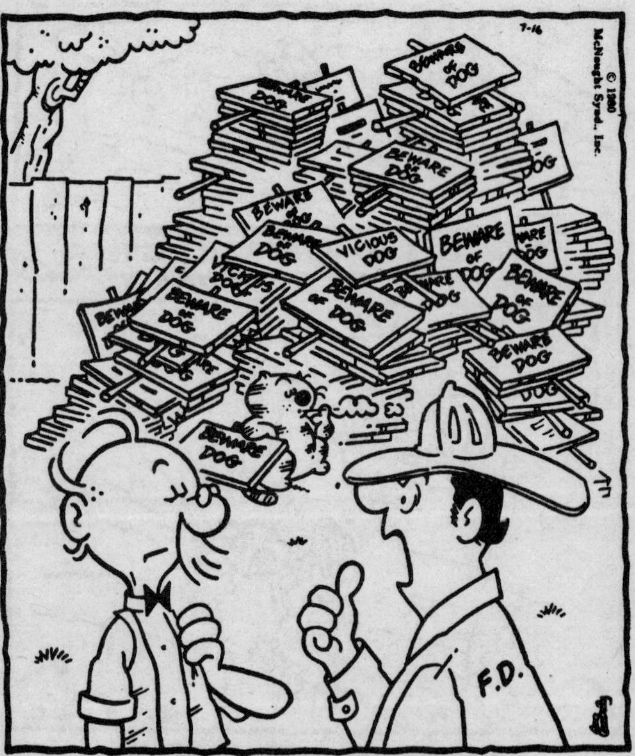

7-16
© 1980 McNaught Synd., Inc.
BEWARE OF DOG
VICIOUS DOG
BEWARE OF DOG
F.D.

"THE CHIEF SAYS HIS COLLECTION CONSTITUTES A FIRE HAZARD."

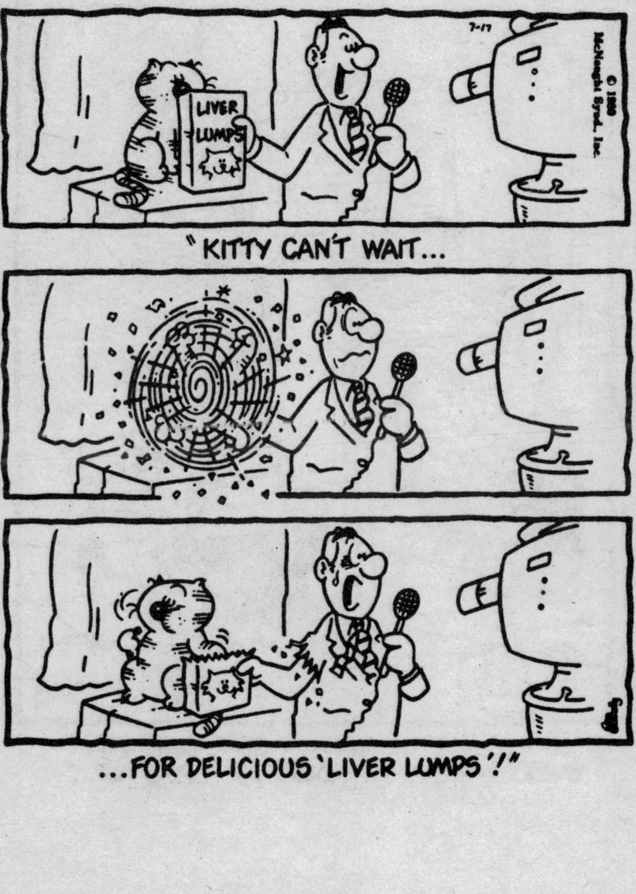
7-17
© 1980 McNaught Synd., Inc.
LIVER LUMPS
"KITTY CAN'T WAIT...
...FOR DELICIOUS 'LIVER LUMPS'!"

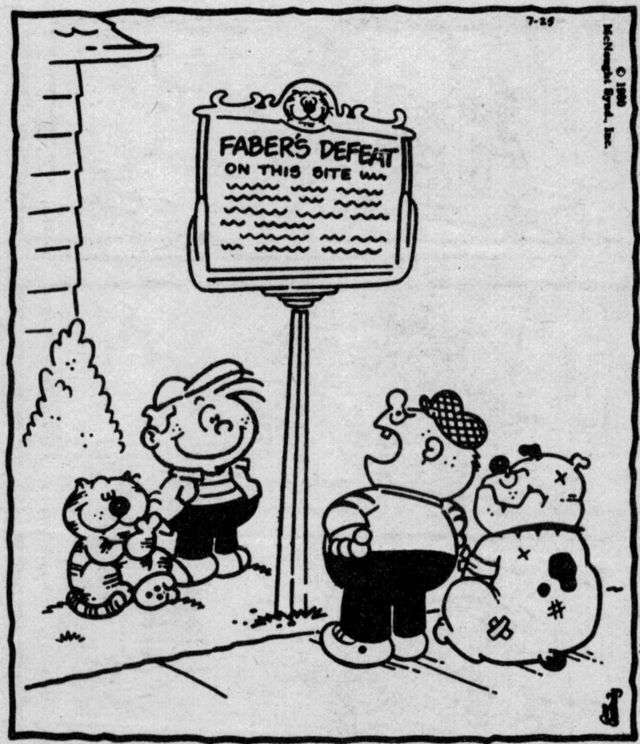
7-29
FABER'S DEFEAT
ON THIS SITE

"ON THIS SITE THE VALIANT HEATHCLIFF DIDST VANQUISH MUGGSY FABER'S DOG SPIKE AND..."

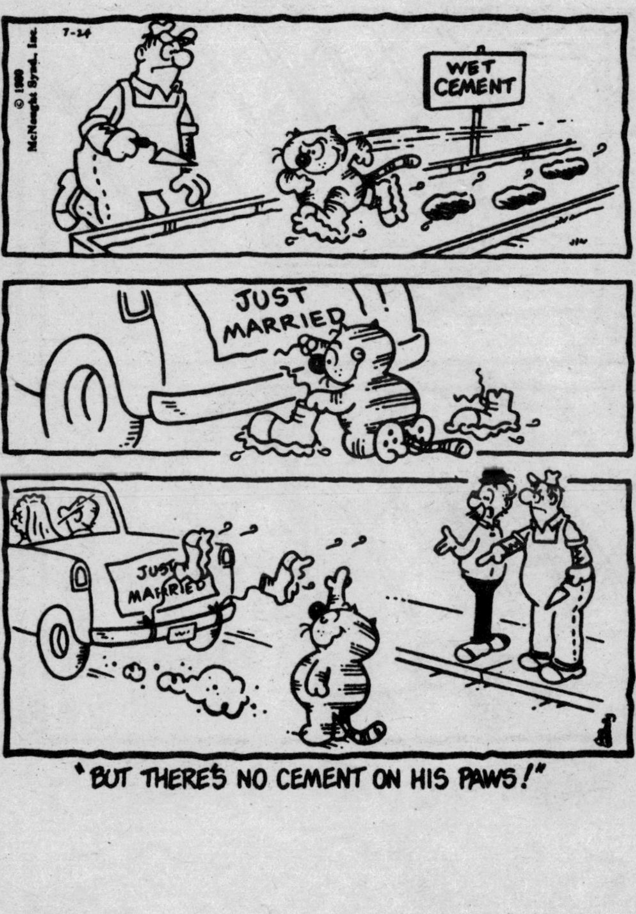
McNaught Synd., Inc.
7-24
WET CEMENT
JUST MARRIED
JUST MARRIED

"BUT THERE'S NO CEMENT ON HIS PAWS!"

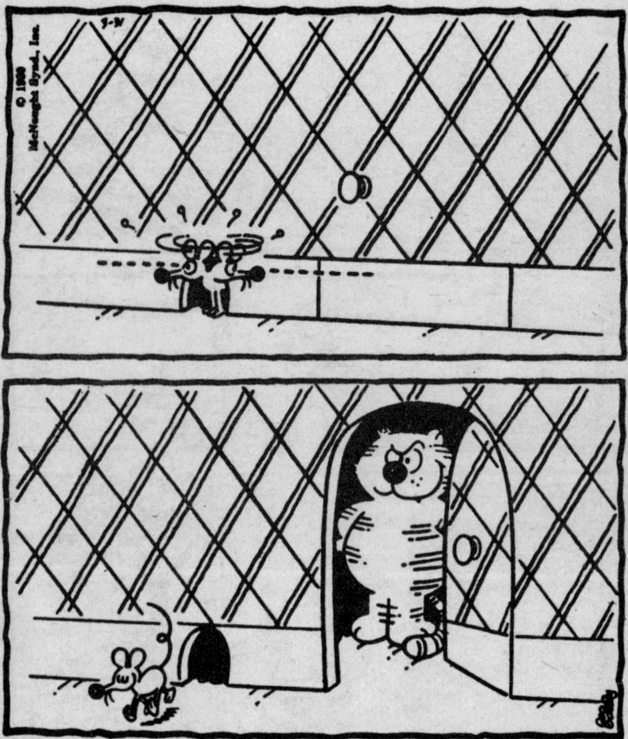
McNaught Synd., Inc.

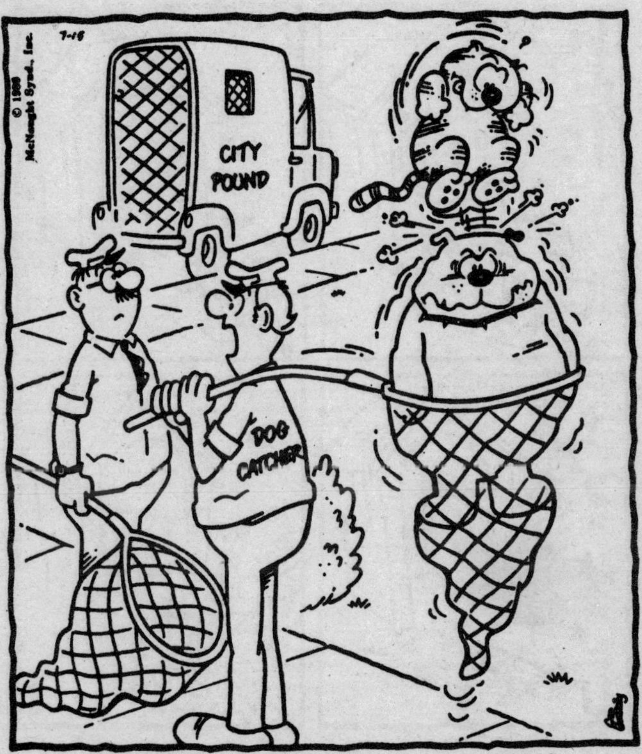
© 1986 McNaught Synd., Inc.
7-18
CITY POUND
DOG CATCHER
"THIS ONE HARDLY FITS IN THE NET!"

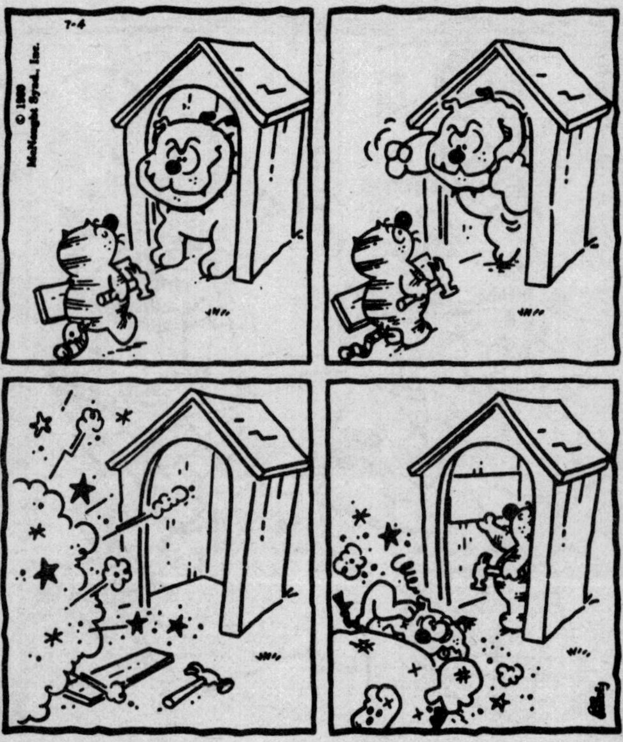
7-4
McNaught Synd., Inc.

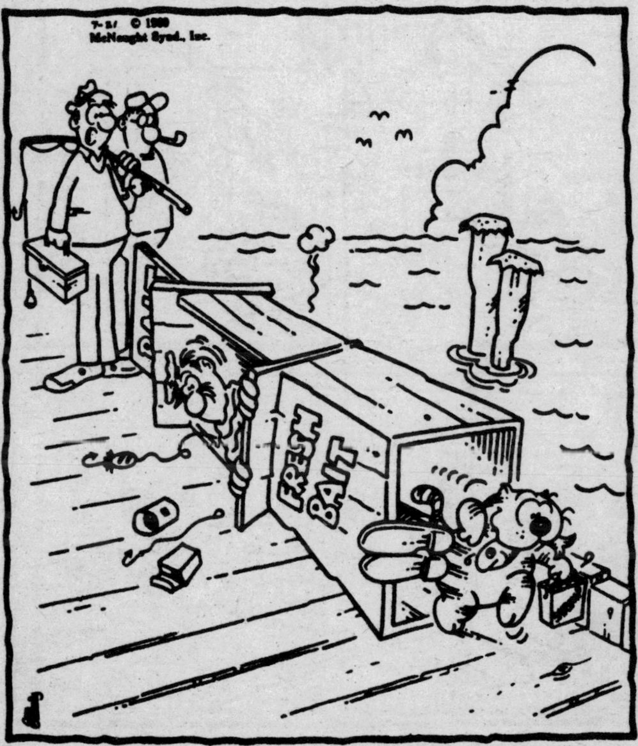
7-21 © 1980
McNaught Synd., Inc.
FRESH BAIT
"SOMEONE KNOCKED OVER THE BAIT SHOP!"

"HE'S WORKING WITH A BEAVER!"